CLEAN COCKTAILS

CLEAN COCKTAILS

Righteous Recipes for the

Modern Mixologist

BETH RITTER NYDICK
and
TARA ROSCIOLI

Photographs by AMY ROTH

THE COUNTRYMAN PRESS
A DIVISION OF W. W. NORTON & COMPANY
Independent Publishers Since 1923

Contents

Meet Your *Tipsy* Fairy Godmothers

Two health coaches walk into a bar . . .
I'm Beth, a former TV producer by day
and bartender by night. I spent five years
in television working 18-hour days trying
to get ahead, fueled with nothing but Diet
Coke and the occasional corn muffin.
To be honest, the sleep deprivation and
Diet Coke addiction made me one hangry
bitch. I barely slept and always felt
terrible. In college, I cured my irritable
bowel syndrome (IBS) by eating "right"
and spent hours in the library reading
books on nutrition and the food system—
but years out of school, I'd landed far away
from where I had begun.

Thankfully, the cancellation of my TV
show in early 2001 forced me to reevaluate
my life and get back on track. When I
became pregnant later that year, I soaked
up any information I could find on what
to eat to prevent my son from developing
food allergies. I made my own baby food
from fresh vegetables I grew myself. The
women in my "mommy group" thought I
was bonkers . . . until they started asking
for my help. They peppered me with
questions like "Beth, what do I do if my
kids won't eat this?" and "How do I make
my own baby food?" I was eager to answer
them. I offered loads of sound advice,
but I still craved more information. This
pursuit of all things healthy led to my
enrollment in the Institute for Integrative
Nutrition and my transformation into

a certified holistic health coach. Since graduating from the program, I've helped hundreds of clients improve their health by changing the way they eat. Food truly is the medicine!

And I'm Tara, a former attorney with a predisposition for cigarettes and Swedish fish. Years of living on nicotine and candy took its toll on me both physically and emotionally. I'd start each day with my Marlboro Lights and a Dunkin' Donuts coffee loaded with skim milk and artificial sweeteners. At lunch, I'd eat like a bird, snacking on fat-free cheese slices and diet bread. For dinner, I'd have a few glasses of wine and iceberg lettuce.

But behind the scenes, I secretly ate bags and bags of candy. In one desperate moment, I even found myself eating jelly beans out of my office wastebasket (P.S.—it was otherwise empty!). There was also the time my 4-year-old son caught me eating candy corn in the dark and asked what I was eating; I lied and told him they were almonds because I didn't want to share.

On the outside, I looked like a relatively thin and fit individual, but on the inside, I was sickly and inflamed. My skin was gray and prone to breakouts. I had dark circles under my eyes, and I barely had the energy to do the things I used to love. I knew I had to make a change, so I decided to leave the law and pursue a more forgiving lifestyle. Like Beth, I enrolled in the Institute for Integrative Nutrition and became a certified holistic health coach. Now, I help other professionals find ways to incorporate healthy eating and exercise into their hectic lives.

Now let's talk about how the two of us met. Flash back a year or so: We're both at a networking event for health coaches at a restaurant that no longer exists. Finding ourselves surrounded by colleagues drinking San Pellegrino and discussing colonics, both of us fled to the bar—desperately in need of a drink. We introduced ourselves and bonded over our drink orders.

"Gin Mojito, no sugar, please," asked Beth.

"Patron Silver over ice with freshly squeezed lime juice, please!" ordered Tara. "No Rose's lime juice."

We clinked glasses and shrugged off the looks the other health coaches shot us. Then we chatted with the bartender, who thought we'd conspired to make his afternoon difficult by ordering off-menu drinks. After some conversation about the need for cleaner cocktail menus, we had him convinced we were on to something. At that moment, at that bar, and over those clean drinks, our idea for *Clean Cocktails: Righteous Recipes for the Modern Mixologist* was born.

Now you may be surprised that two certified holistic health coaches (not to mention suburban moms) would drink alcohol beyond the occasional glass of wine with dinner. Frankly, we often feel the bitter sting of judgment from our peers in the wellness industry when they hear about our girls' nights out. While our boozy ways may seem like a contradiction to clean living, drinking doesn't have to be dirty—at least not when the cocktails are made with the freshest fruits, herbs, spices, and gentle sweeteners.

So why should you care about any of this? Well, think about it—gluten-free, dairy-free, and refined sugar-free foods are all the rage these days, and most restaurants have menus that accommodate those dietary restrictions. Yet any time we order a cocktail without sugar, bartenders question their hearing and our sanity.

So in a world where seemingly everyone is clean-eating conscious, why are they drinking dirty cocktails loaded with refined sugar, artificial flavors, and dyes? The artificial mixers and additives found in the average cocktail, which we consider a "chemical shitstorm," are what are causing your headaches, bloat, and overall inflammation—you know, the typical hangover!

So is all that enough reason for you to ditch crazy-colored drinks that are loaded with sugar? How about this—according to the Center for Drug Design at the University of Minnesota, artificial food colors and flavoring have been linked to mood swings, sleep disturbances, asthma, and diabetes, and they may play a role in the development of Alzheimer's or Parkinson's disease. Now are you convinced?

Well, after years of playing in our home bars, we're happy to teach the I'd-rather-do-it-myself generation how to booze it up the healthy way. Crafted for the millions who invest in their health and wellness, *Clean Cocktails: Righteous Recipes for the Modern Mixologist* is the resource guide on all-things-cocktail for those who still want to enjoy a drink without undoing all their hard work at the gym or dinner table.

Our philosophy in creating this guide was to use four popular low-calorie spirits that pair beautifully with a wide array of flavor palates to build exceptional cocktails made with freshly expressed or freshly squeezed fruit and vegetable juices and purees packed with vitamins; fresh herbs containing loads of nutrients; and spices known to reduce inflammation, such as cinnamon, cayenne pepper, and ginger. Unlike traditional recipes, which are full of refined sugars, our clean recipes use natural, gentle sweeteners like honey and dates (and many others), as they create less of a spike in blood-sugar levels and cause fewer headaches the morning after. These whole-fruit and whole-vegetable juices and purees, fresh herbs, and spices, along with our own collections of customized bitters and clean and natural syrups, are the very essence of *Clean Cocktails: Righteous Recipes for the Modern Mixologist*.

It's important to remember that alcohol should always be enjoyed responsibly. Excessive consumption of alcohol of any kind—even if it comes in the form of clean cocktails—is hazardous to your health. *Cheers!*

Love,

Your Tipsy Fairy Godmothers

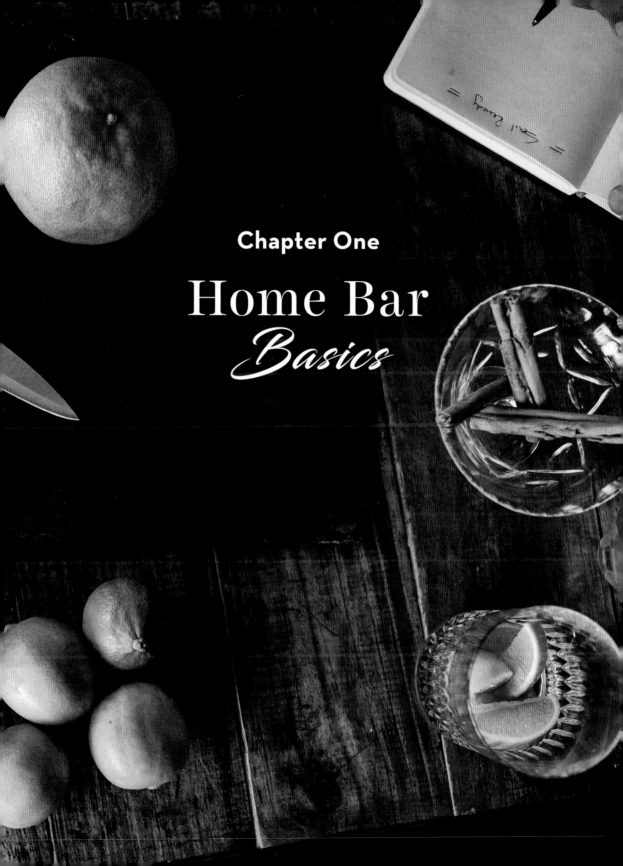

Chapter One

Home Bar
Basics

THE BUZZ:
Stocking Your Bar

We've created our recipes using vodka, gin, tequila, and bourbon, very popular liquors that you're likely to have on hand. While these liquor options are low in both calories (roughly 96 calories per 1½ ounces) and carbohydrates, we've really selected these four because they pair beautifully with vitamin-packed fresh fruit and vegetable juices, gentle sweeteners like honey that have reduced effects on blood-sugar levels, and anti-inflammatory spices like cinnamon, cayenne pepper, and ginger. The unique combinations of these liquors and healthy, real-food ingredients is the essence of a clean cocktail. There's nothing quite like sipping on a guilt-free cocktail . . . or two. It's important to remember, however, that even clean cocktails should be enjoyed in moderation.

VA VA VA VODKA

"When life hands you lemons, make lemonade with vodka."
—CHELSEA HANDLER

Vodka, how do we love thee? Let us count the ways. Whether we enjoy you in a cool and refreshing cocktail après work or as part of our Sunday-morning "hair of the dog," you never disappoint. Vodka . . . because no good story starts with "that one time I ate salad."

As it's relatively neutral in flavor, vodka is a great choice when you're looking to pair something with a favorite clean mixer. As we mentioned, vodka is waistline friendly and goes well with freshly squeezed (never from concentrate) fruit juices, veggie purees (think cucumbers), and splashes of seltzer water for minimal additional calories.

Vodka is made by distilling grains, such as rye, wheat, and even quinoa. It can also be produced by distilling potatoes or corn in regions where such crops are prevalent. Vodka can even be made from fruits, like grapes. Vodka is our number one here, not only because of its low calorie count but also because several major brands offer gluten-free varieties.

Now here's the skinny on vodka: We have heard tell that drinking vodka in moderation can be a smart choice when following a sensible weight-loss

program. We have not seen scientific proof of this, but if the shoe fits (or if the jeans fit), we might have a second cocktail.

FOR THE GIN RATS

"I exercise strong self-control. I never drink anything stronger than gin before breakfast."

—ANONYMOUS

Gin is made of juniper berries. Juniper berries are fruit. Fruit is good for you. Therefore, gin is good for you. . . .

Okay, so maybe this is a game we like to play with ourselves. Gin is another great choice when you're looking to build a smarter cocktail. Of additional interest: Juniper berries, the main ingredient in gin, have become a popular supplement for combating infections. We're not really suggesting that drinking gin is good for you, but it doesn't hurt to know that it's created from a food with healthful qualities. It's also true that gin pairs beautifully with fresh citrus fruits packed with vitamin C, such as grapefruits and limes, and herbs that promote digestion, such as mint. With all this taken into consideration, gin ranks as one of our favorites.

Unlike vodka, gin is defined by its taste. A good gin has a botanical flavor, like juniper berries, but distillers often add citrus notes, spices, and nuts to diversify its taste. We'll drink to that!

TEQUILA SUNRISE AND SUNSET

"We should all believe in something. I believe it's time for another shot of tequila."

—JUSTIN TIMBERLAKE

For many, the thought of tequila calls to mind slammers, shooters, body shots, and other questionable spring break activities. We get it! We abstained from drinking tequila for years after college. But in the last few years, tequila has gained popularity at our cocktail parties. As it contains no added sugars, tequila is a great base for a clean craft cocktail—and that's without taking into consideration that *everyone* is crazy fun on tequila! Stick with blanco or silver tequilas, which are less likely to contain acetone or tannins than darker liquors.

Tequila is delicious when complemented with simple flavors, such as freshly squeezed lime juice, a clean cucumber puree, or an unexpected kick of chili powder. Ah, hell—tequila is great straight up.

Tequila comes from the blue agave plant, but don't confuse that with agave nectar, a highly processed sweetener much like high-fructose corn syrup. Tequilas can differ in color and taste depending on their maturation processes and the types of wood used for aging. We personally prefer the flavor of silver or white tequila, which is why we recommend it in our recipes. If you prefer gold tequila, please feel free to swap it in.

Some people say that tequila can help stave off illness during cold and flu season, as the agave in tequila (again, not agave nectar) can tame a sore throat and kill bacteria. We've also read about a study that found that people aged 75 and older who drink tequila regularly may be less likely to develop dementia. But, really, the best reason to drink it is that everyone is crazy fun on tequila.

Of course, before you decide to trade in your flu vaccine for a margarita bender, please remember that these studies are merely anecdotal.

BRINGING BOURBON TO THE 'BURBS

"Mr. Bourbon and Coke laugh at all my jokes."
—BLAKE SHELTON

Bourbon may remind you of nights gone wrong or perhaps a few poor life choices. Call us "old fashioned," but bourbon reminds *us* of our granddaddies and simpler times, when a proper drink made everything seem better.

All bourbon is whiskey, but not all whiskey is bourbon. Did we lose you there? Whiskies are typically made from barley and rye, but bourbon, a type of whiskey, is produced only in the United States and must be distilled from at least 51 percent corn.

Bourbon is characterized by undertones of vanilla, caramel, and toasted oak. It's enjoyed neat (without ice or mixers), on the rocks (over ice), or in cocktails, such as Manhattans and Whiskey Sours. These cocktails—like many favorites—are loaded with refined sugars that overwhelm the natural flavor of the bourbon, instead of enhancing it. Instead, make yourself a glass of SuBourbon Problems (see page 89) or one of our other bourbon cocktail recipes, and you'll benefit from the flavorful, gut-healthy bitters it contains. Soon enough, you'll understand how bourbon has earned its place in *Clean Cocktails: Righteous Recipes for the Modern Mixologist.*

RAISING THE BAR:
How to Make Your Home Bar Work for You

Shakers, strainers, rimmers—OH MY! There's an overwhelming number of tools to choose from when building your bar, but you really need only a few key utensils and techniques to make your own clean cocktails. On the pages that follow, we identify which are must-haves and which you can skimp on, and we also identify a few of our favorite playthings for already-savvy mixologists who want to up their game.

THE TOOLS

SHAKERS. Think of the cocktail shaker as your magic cauldron. Every mixologist needs a good shaker with a tight-fitting lid that's able to protect their rugs and their guests' clothing. Trust us when we say you don't want to skimp here! We recommend a **Boston shaker**, which includes a metal canister and a pint glass that covers and seals (that's the operative word here!) the canister very effectively. The Boston shaker is simple to use, but it will require you to purchase a Hawthorne strainer (see page 9) to separate muddled fruits and herbs from your cocktails—unless you want to spend the evening picking basil from your teeth. The **cobbler shaker**, on the other hand, is a confusing little contraption. The cobbler shaker has three pieces: a metal container, a metal lid with a built-in strainer, and also a metal cap to cover the strainer. That's a lot of pieces to keep track of! Just try using a cobbler shaker without the cap (#notadvised), and the cobbler can be difficult to open once it's cold. We suggest going with the Boston shaker—it's wicked cool!

STRAINERS. Your best bet when building your own bar is to invest in a **Hawthorne strainer**. While they're not the easiest to clean, these springy bad boys easily adapt to fit any size cup or glass, ensuring a spill-proof fit. Plus, your friends will be impressed that you own this nifty little tool. A **julep strainer** is easy to work with and even easier to clean, but we think it's a bit sloppy to use. In a pinch, a fine mesh strainer will do the trick, and you probably already have one in your kitchen.

BAR SPOONS. Bar spoons are a necessary alternative to a cocktail shaker when your drink needs to be stirred, not shaken. Purchase a few long-handled metal bar spoons for blending spirits and mixers in tall glasses or containers.

MUDDLERS. There are SO many options, but we don't want to muddle the waters, so let's cut right to the chase. If you're a newbie mixologist, go with a plastic-tipped, lightly textured muddler that's versatile and easy to work with. Wooden muddler handles are easy to hold, but wood is porous and won't withstand multiple rounds in your dishwasher. Plastic, which is nonporous and dishwasher safe, is a better and more durable option. Once you've graduated to higher mixology skills, you can play around with muddlers with smoother or rougher tips and those made with other materials.

JIGGERS. This handy little two-sided (larger side, 1½ ounces; smaller side, ¾ ounce) steel measure ensures precision when building your clean cocktails, and it's a good idea to use one if you happen to be a mixologist with a heavy pour. If you don't happen to have a jigger, a favorite shot glass from your college days can also keep you in check.

CITRUS PRESSES. While it's not absolutely essential, you'll find that a handheld citrus juice press is extremely useful when making clean cocktails.

(We're talking fresh here, people!) Perfect for extracting the juice of lemons and limes, this easy-to-use tool keeps the seeds out of your sangria. Of course, you'll need something larger if working with oranges or grapefruits.

JUICER. So that citrus press will not get you very far when making cocktails requiring fresh vegetable purees or even the juices of watermelon, cantaloupe, and such. For this, you will need a small juicer to separate the fresh juice from the fiber and pulp of your fruits and vegetables. Keep it small and simple—you won't need an expensive or fancy model to achieve your goal.

ZESTER/GRATERS. You'll need this for freshly grated spices like nutmeg and ginger and also for removing zest from citrus fruits. A small zester is the best choice, but in a pinch you can use the small outward-facing spikes on a regular cheese grater. Either way, watch your fingers!

MEASURING CUPS. Any old set of measuring cups will do, but we recommend using a set with spouts for easier pouring.

KNIVES AND CUTTING BOARDS. There are definitely many cool cocktail knives on the market for slicing fruit and garnishes, but we think any paring knife you already have in your kitchen will do. You'll use the knife for cutting lime and lemon wheels, fruit wedges, and swaths of citrus zest for twisting over cocktails. Looking to snazz up your cocktail game? A **channel knife** will make those long, curly pieces of citrus zest a snap.

THE TECHNIQUES

So you have the freshest ingredients and the proper tools at your fingertips. Now what? Those cocktails won't make themselves! Don't panic—this is the fun part. With these few techniques and a little bit of practice, you'll be comfortable entertaining in no time.

CHILL. Chilling glasses is simple: just pop the glasses you'll be using in the fridge or freezer for 20 minutes before use. If you forget, fill the glasses with ice while you're mixing the drinks and dump out the ice before you pour.

RIM. Rimming is the art of creating a very tasty accent on the lip of a glass. A proper rim will complement and enhance the flavor of your cocktail. To rim a glass, place the elements of the rim—let's say kosher salt or coconut sugar—on a plate. Moisten the outside rim of the glass with a lime wedge (if working with the salt) or an orange or lemon wedge (if working with the coconut sugar). Then, dip the rim of the glass in the salt or sugar until it's coated. Do your best not to coat the inside of the glass . . . you don't want the excess to land in your cocktail and ruin the taste of your drink.

GARNISH. Garnishing drinks isn't just about aesthetics. Garnishes allow you to enhance your drink, adding layers and textures, with the zests or peels of fruits and vegetables and the stems and leaves of herbs. We always feel proud when we use all the parts of our recipes' ingredients and leave little waste.

JUICE. Always use freshly squeezed or freshly expressed fruit juices, thus ensuring that there are no added sugars or preservatives in your cocktails. You'll also save money by avoiding expensive, name-brand bottles of juice that are loaded with additives. To use a handheld citrus press, slice the fruit in half, open the press's handles, and place the half cut-side down in the bowl of the press. Close the handles and squeeze firmly, making sure to turn the press over to release any remaining juice. Choose fruits with shiny peels; the shine indicates that their skins are thin and that they are likely to yield more juice. Keep your fruits at room temperature before juicing, as cold fruits are harder to work with. Just before juicing, roll the fruit on a clean surface to loosen up its fibers. Then you can go to town!

MUDDLE. Muddling involves mashing or jumbling ingredients together. Put a plastic, wooden, or even metal muddler to good use by pushing down and twisting on ingredients— perhaps fresh fruits or herbs—to release the oils and juices that

are trapped within their leaves or rinds and add layers of flavor to your drink. Put a little elbow grease in there . . . don't be shy!

To **muddle** fruits, herbs, and spices, place them in a sturdy mixing glass and, using the muddler, firmly press down and twist to gently release the flavors of the chosen ingredients. Muddling fruit always requires more twists than herbs. The goal is to release the essence of the ingredients—not to pulverize them.

SHAKE. Shaking, plain and simple, is the primary way to mix and chill cocktail ingredients, and it's the preferred method of your tipsy fairy godmothers. To properly shake a cocktail, fill the mixing glass of a Boston shaker halfway with ice. Add the cocktail ingredients and clamp the metal container onto the mixing glass, ensuring that it is well sealed. Shake for 10 seconds. Use a strainer to separate out any solids or contents that don't belong in your drink (like muddled fruits and herbs, or ice in a drink served up) and pour the contents of the shaker into a chilled cocktail or martini glass.

STIR. Stirring, the alternative to shaking, is typically the means by which ingredients are mixed in drinks served in highball or rocks glasses, Mason jars, or copper mule mugs. While shaking chills and dilutes a drink by moving it swiftly around in the shaker with ice, stirring a drink with a long, metal bar spoon better maintains the spirits' flavor.

STRAIN. Straining separates fruits, herbs, and ice from your cocktail when pouring a drink from a shaker or a pitcher to a glass.

TWIST. Twisting involves passing a twist (a long, curly strand of fruit zest) over the rim of the glass and then dropping it over the drink to accent it with a hint of flavor from the zest's oil.

THE GOODS AND THE GARNISH: Looks Count!

The trademark of a great cocktail is its aesthetics. A fabulous craft cocktail should be visually pleasing and, occasionally, unexpected. It should evoke

a mood, and sipping on it should be an experience.

In this section, we introduce some of the ingredients necessary to create such a visual, flavorful experience: fresh fruits, such as lemons, limes, oranges, berries, and melons; fresh vegetables, such as cucumbers, tomatoes (red, yellow, and green), celery, bell peppers, and jalapeños; fresh herbs, such as mint, sage, basil, rosemary, thyme, and cilantro; favorite cocktail accessories, such as olives, wasabi, and seltzer; and the unexpected, like ginger, cinnamon, chili powder, vanilla, matcha tea powder, cardamom, star anise, and unsweetened coconut.

HERBS. Add freshness, flavor, and color to your cocktails with the addition of herbs such as mint, rosemary, basil, and sage.

INFUSED SALTS AND SUGARS. For a treat, make your own infused salts and sugars. In a food processor, grind together coarse sea salt and lime zest or coconut sugar and orange or lemon zest for an extra-special addition to your cocktail experience. We also love a touch of celery

sea salt in our clean versions of the Bloody Mary: the Bloody SophistiKATEd (see page 135), the Wasabi Mary (see page 141), and the Verde Mary (see page 147).

PEEL. Use a paring knife or other sharp knife to cut an oval shape out of a fruit's skin, taking care to avoid the bitter pith. Rub the peel around the rim of your glass to add a hint of citrus flavor to your cocktail.

TWIST. Use a paring knife or other sharp knife to cut off both ends of a fruit and then remove the skin carefully in a long, thin piece—again avoiding the pith. Once it has been removed, roll the skin into a twist that looks pretty and gives off a great aroma.

WEDGE. Use a paring knife to slice a lemon, lime, or orange into eighths.

WHEEL. Use a paring knife to slice citrus fruits into perfect circles or carrots and ginger into coins, and give each a slit halfway through so it can sit pretty on the rim of a glass.

GLASSES HALF FULL: Pairing the Right Glass with the Right Cocktail

If you think it's acceptable to drink out of a Solo cup, you're wrong (unless you're playing a game of beer pong, of course!). We're excited to share with you why certain glasses and cocktails are paired to complement or enhance the clean craft cocktail experience. Sure, appearances matter—but did you know that enjoying a cocktail in the correct glass increases its taste tenfold? Consider this your form-meets-function tutorial for glassware. But if the thought of hosting your own cocktail party gives you heart palpitations, relax! We're going to break this down for you into must-haves and optional glassware choices, and explain why certain glasses are best for particular cocktails.

THE RIGHT STUFF

HIGHBALL GLASS. Typically ranging in size from 8 to 12 ounces, this tall glass is ideal for drinks that contain a greater percentage of non-alcoholic ingredients, such as fruit juices and seltzers. Great for drinks served with ice, highballs streamline carbonation (don't ask us how) and therefore work very well for any cocktail containing seltzer or soda water.

ROCKS (AKA LOWBALL OR TUMBLER) GLASS. This is also great for cocktails served with ice. A rocks glass, which typically ranges in size from 4 to 8 ounces, is a short and stout vessel designed for large ice cubes. Like the highball, the rocks glass is designed for building drinks right in the glass. Note, however, that we sometimes still shake the cocktails we serve in rocks glasses, usually because we often include muddled herbs and spices in our recipes. Be sure to strain solids out of your drinks, because it's hard to look good with a piece of mint stuck between your front teeth.

MARTINI (AKA COCKTAIL) GLASS.

What could be more glam than a gorgeous, triangular glass with a long, slender stem? Skip the stemless martini glasses! They may be cute, but the very important stem on a classic martini glass allows you to hold your cocktail without warming it and thus interfering with its delicious flavor. The martini glass's wide opening allows you to enjoy the cocktail's aroma before the very first taste—consider it foreplay, if you will. Choose a smaller-sized martini glass to ensure that every last sip is fresh and chilled. Have your shaker and strainer at the ready, because you'll need both to create delicious martinis.

A FEW FUN ADDITIONS

MASON JAR. We typically use Mason jars for storing our delicious homemade syrups and bitters because of their airtight lids. But they're useful in other ways—Mason jars also make a rustic presentation as a drinking glass, and they're perfect for summer barbecues or picnics.

COPPER MUG. The beautiful thing about the copper mug, other than its distinctive color and attractive appearance, is that it insulates its contents, keeping your drink cool or hot. Many vodka drinks, such as the popular Moscow Mule, are served in copper mugs. We never met a mule (or a copper mug) we didn't like.

MARGARITA/COUPETTE GLASS.

Like the cocktail glass, the margarita or coupette glass has a wide mouth that allows the drinker to enjoy the cocktail's aroma before taking a sip. Choose smaller glasses for drinks without ice and larger ones for frozen drinks. Random cocktail fact: some say the original coupette glass was molded from the breast of Marie Antoinette. We say, "Let them drink clean cocktails!"

P.S. Bigger isn't always better. Can we be honest? Unless you're in your 20s, you don't need a 16-ounce martini glass! When in doubt, select 6-ounce glasses for your bar. They're stylish and classic, and your guests' cocktails will always stay fresh until they're gone. And then you can serve them another.

Chapter Two

Bitters *and* Syrups

IT'S BITTERSWEET: Making Your Own Bitters and Clean Syrups

Here, we'll teach you how to make your own clean and "simple" syrups using gentle sweeteners like honey, dates, coconut sugar, and maple syrup. Since they contain more natural, and less refined, sweeteners, our cocktails don't impact blood-sugar levels the way those made with simple syrups and pre-packaged mixes do.

We'll also show you how to make bitters by infusing distilled alcohol with seeds, fruit peels, roots, beans, and other natural ingredients. While syrups gently sweeten cocktails, bitters add body, zest, and a little zing to your drinks. Booyah!

CLEAN SYRUPS

It's time to have a little fun in the kitchen. With a few whole and simple ingredients and a bit of prep time, you can create a wide array of delicious syrups that are perfect for long-term storage (so they're there for your next cocktail party).

Rather than using simple syrups, which are made with refined sugar, we have created our own syrup recipes sweetened with honey, ginger, coconut, and pure maple syrup—healthier alternatives. While these "gentle" sweeteners aren't calorie-free, they are less refined, come from more natural sources, contain a wide array of nutrients, and are easy to make at home.

We regularly use Mason jars to store our syrups so we can see exactly what we're pulling from the refrigerator, and as an added benefit, their tight-fitting lids keep the syrups fresh for months. We also recommend slapping labels on your Mason jars that list the type of syrup and the date prepared, so you always know what's what.

Basil *Syrup* MAKES APPROXIMATELY 1 TO 1¼ CUPS

Eating fresh basil gives your immunity a boost, so why shouldn't your cocktails pack the same punch? This simple recipe adds a clean and pleasant flavor to your cocktails with minimal calories. Try Basil Syrup in the Basilrita (see page 65), Drunken Gardener (see page 143), and Caprese Cocktail (see page 148) recipes.

1 cup honey

1 cup filtered water

1 cup fresh basil leaves

One 1-pint Mason jar

Combine all of the ingredients in a medium pot over medium-high heat and bring to a boil. Reduce the heat to low and simmer, stirring constantly, until the honey has completely dissolved. Remove from the heat and set aside to allow the syrup to steep for 1 hour.

Once the syrup has cooled, strain out and discard the basil leaves. Transfer the syrup to the Mason jar, ensure the seal is airtight, and store in the refrigerator.

> Basil Syrup will keep in the refrigerator sealed in an airtight Mason jar for 1 to 2 months.

Cinnamon Girl *Syrup*

MAKES APPROXIMATELY 1 TO 1¼ CUPS

We could be happy for the rest of our lives with this Cinnamon Girl Syrup. This gentle sweetener has a warm, spicy note that pairs well with tea and coffee. The combination of honey and cinnamon boosts your body's immune and digestive systems, and it may even stimulate weight loss. (Hey, one can hope!) Together, these two powerhouses contain the vitamins and minerals you need to maintain good health. Try Cinnamon Girl Syrup in the Cold Fashioned (see page 48) and Steep Thoughts (see page 186) recipes.

1 cup filtered water

2 cinnamon sticks

1 cup honey

One 1-pint Mason jar

Combine the water and cinnamon sticks in a small saucepan over medium-high heat and bring to a boil. Remove from the heat and set aside for 10 minutes.

Add the honey and stir until the honey is dissolved. Set aside to cool for 1 hour.

Once it has cooled, transfer the syrup to the Mason jar, ensure the seal is airtight, and store in the refrigerator.

> Cinnamon Girl Syrup will keep in the refrigerator sealed in an airtight Mason jar for up to 3 months. Make sure to remove and discard the cinnamon sticks before your first use.

Coconut *Syrup*   MAKES APPROXIMATELY 1 TO 1¼ CUPS

Made from the sap of the coconut blossom, coconut sugar is the sweetener we use most often, as it is less refined and comes from a sustainable source. Our Coconut Syrup is loaded with vitamins B and C and is ridiculously simple to make. Try Coconut Syrup in the Coconut-Cucumber Margarita (see page 70), Three-Tequila-Floor Sangria (see page 81), and Fertile Blond (see page 86) recipes.

1 cup filtered water

2 cups coconut sugar

One 1-pint Mason jar

Place the water in a medium pot over medium-high heat and bring to a rolling boil. Add the coconut sugar and reduce the heat to low. Simmer, stirring occasionally, for approximately 6 to 8 minutes (the mixture will reduce by one-third). Remove from the heat and set aside to cool for 1 hour.

Once it has cooled, transfer the syrup to the Mason jar, ensure the seal is airtight, and store in the refrigerator.

> Coconut Syrup will keep in the refrigerator sealed in an airtight Mason jar for up to 3 months.

Date *Syrup*   MAKES APPROXIMATELY 1¼ TO 1½ CUPS

Dates offer a warmer and nuttier flavor than other sweeteners. We found that dates offer a moderate level of sweetness that is ideal for use in cocktails. Dates are a wonderful addition to your kitchen or home bar as they are high in vitamins and minerals and loaded with fiber, which promotes digestive health. Try Date Syrup in the "Dated" Old Fashioned (see page 51) recipe.

20 to 25 Medjool dates, pitted

3 cups filtered water

One 1-pint Mason jar

Combine the dates and water in a medium pot over medium-high heat and bring to a boil.

Smash the dates with the back of a wooden spoon to break them down. Reduce the heat to low and simmer for 30 to 40 minutes. Remove from the heat and set aside to cool for 1 hour.

Pour the contents through a strainer and into a bowl, using a wooden spoon to press down on the dates and release any remaining liquid.

Once it has been strained, transfer the syrup to the Mason jar, ensure the seal is airtight, and store in the refrigerator.

> Date Syrup will keep in the refrigerator sealed in an airtight Mason jar for up to 1 month.
>
> Dates are loaded with potassium, copper, iron, and vitamin B6. Dates may be helpful in reducing LDL cholesterol (the bad kind).

Ginger *Syrup* MAKES APPROXIMATELY 1¼ TO 1½ CUPS

This sweet and spicy syrup is a delicious addition to your cocktails—and rather tasty on your morning pancakes, we might add. Ginger should be a staple in both your kitchen and your medicine cabinet, as it is a well-known remedy for nausea and alleviates symptoms of the common cold. We love using Ginger Syrup in the We Got the Beet (see page 136) and Kiwi Punch (see page 181) recipes.

1 cup peeled and sliced fresh ginger *×2 = 2cups*

2 thick lemon slices *×2 = 4slices*

¾ cup raw honey *×2 = 1½ cup*

1½ cups filtered water *×2 = 3cups*

One 1-pint Mason jar

Combine all of the ingredients in a medium saucepan over medium-high heat, stirring until honey is dissolved, and then bring to a boil. Remove from the heat and set aside, covered, for 1 hour and 15 minutes to allow the syrup to steep.

Once the syrup has cooled, strain out and discard the ginger and lemon slices. Transfer the syrup to the Mason jar, ensure the seal is airtight, and store in the refrigerator.

> Ginger Syrup will keep in the refrigerator sealed in an airtight Mason jar for up to 3 months.
>
> Ginger, a versatile spice, adds flavor and flair to cocktails. A powerhouse packed with healing abilities, ginger helps with the digestion process and combats nausea and inflammation. Keep Ginger Syrup in your refrigerator for a cocktail or even mixed with a cup of tea for when you're feeling under the weather.

Honey *Syrup*   MAKES APPROXIMATELY 1¼ TO 1½ CUPS

If you make only one syrup for your home bar, our Honey Syrup should be it!
The combination of minerals, vitamins, and amino acids in honey is unlike that
of any other sweetener on the planet. While honey is high in fructose and can
elevate blood-sugar levels, it is also loaded with antioxidants that prevent disease.
We recommend using darker honeys, as they are even richer in minerals and
antioxidants. Try Honey Syrup in our Cooling Cucumber Mojito (see page 73),
Garden State (see page 132), Serenity Cocktail (see page 157), and El Chapo (see
page 158) recipes.

---

1 cup raw honey

1 cup filtered water

One 1-pint Mason jar

Combine the honey and water in a medium pot over
medium-high heat and bring to a boil. Reduce the heat
to low and simmer, stirring constantly, until the honey
has completely dissolved. Remove from the heat and
set aside for 1 hour to allow the syrup to steep.

Once it has cooled, transfer the syrup to the Mason
jar, ensure the seal is airtight, and store in the
refrigerator.

> Honey Syrup will keep in the refrigerator sealed
> in an airtight Mason jar for up to 3 months.
>
> Raw honey is loaded with enzymes, antioxidants,
> iron, zinc, potassium, calcium, phosphorous,
> vitamin B6, riboflavin, and niacin. It is important
> to remember that this information applies only
> to raw honey—once it is pasteurized, honey loses
> many of its natural health benefits. While honey
> is high in caloric content, just like sugar, you
> should always choose honey over refined sugar.

Jalapeño *Syrup*   MAKES APPROXIMATELY 1 CUP

We love the sweet and spicy quality of this syrup, as well as its lasting complexity and the kick it adds to our cocktails. Moreover, the capsaicin that gives the jalapeño pepper its heat also stimulates your metabolism and may be helpful in weight loss. Who can say no to that? We love Jalapeño Syrup in The Kiss (see page 123) and Jalapeño Thai Iced Tea (see page 179) recipes.

½ cup honey

½ cup filtered water

1 halved jalapeño pepper, seeds removed

One 1-pint Mason jar

Combine all of the ingredients in a medium pot over medium-high heat and bring to a boil. Reduce the heat to low and simmer, stirring constantly, until the honey has completely dissolved. Remove from the heat and set aside for 1 hour to allow the syrup to steep.

Once the syrup has cooled, strain out and discard the jalapeño pepper. Transfer the syrup to the Mason jar, ensure the seal is airtight, and store in the refrigerator.

Jalapeño Syrup will keep in the refrigerator sealed in an airtight Mason jar for 2 to 4 weeks.

Matcha Tea *Syrup* MAKES APPROXIMATELY ¾ CUP

Matcha tea powder adds a pleasant, earthy flavor to cocktails and contains important vitamins, minerals, and antioxidants that are known to prevent cancer and heart disease. Plus, it's terrific drizzled over ice cream or frozen yogurt. Our Matcha Tea Syrup is amazing in the One Hot Matcha (see page 114) and Orange We a Matcha* (see page 176) recipes.

½ cup filtered water

¼ cup coconut sugar

1½ tablespoons matcha tea powder

One 1-pint Mason jar

*For Orange Matcha Syrup, which provides an extra kick of vitamin C, add ¼ cup freshly squeezed orange juice with the water and coconut sugar.

Combine the water and coconut sugar in a medium pot over medium-high heat and bring to a boil. Continue boiling, stirring constantly, for approximately 5 minutes, until the sugar dissolves.

Remove from the heat and gradually whisk in the matcha tea powder. Set aside to cool for 1 hour.

Once it has cooled, transfer the syrup to the Mason jar, ensure the seal is airtight, and store in the refrigerator.

> Matcha Tea Syrup will keep in the refrigerator sealed in an airtight Mason jar for 1 month.
>
> Matcha, a green tea powder that's gaining in popularity, has enormous anti-inflammatory and energy-enhancing properties. It also helps to cleanse the body of toxins. This Matcha Tea Syrup infuses your cocktails with earthy flavors that pair perfectly with botanicals. Your body will love the side effects.

ary *Syrup* MAKES APPROXIMATELY 2/3 TO 1 CUP

·y is one of the most versatile herbs out there, as it can provide
uniqu~~~~ to everything from cocktails to baked goods. This fragrant syrup
contains plenty of vitamins and minerals—particularly magnesium, calcium,
and iron. Try this syrup in the Sludgehammer (see page 154) and Rosemary
Greyhound (see page 175) recipes.

---

1 cup filtered water

½ cup organic pure maple syrup

4 fresh rosemary sprigs

One 1-pint Mason jar

Combine all of the ingredients in a medium pot over medium-high heat and bring to a boil. Reduce the heat to low and simmer, stirring constantly, until the maple syrup has completely dissolved. Remove from the heat and set aside for 1 hour to allow the syrup to steep.

Once the syrup has cooled, strain out and discard the rosemary. Transfer the syrup to the Mason jar, ensure the seal is airtight, and store in the refrigerator.

> **Rosemary Syrup will keep in the refrigerator sealed in an airtight Mason jar for 3 weeks.**

Vanilla *Syrup* MAKES APPROXIMATELY 1¼ TO 1½ CUPS

This golden-brown caramel syrup has a deep and multifaceted flavor profile that lends itself best to cocktails and baked goods. The medicinal purposes of vanilla, which include anti-inflammatory and cancer-fighting properties, have been known to ancient civilizations for a millennium. Try this syrup in the Twisted (see page 53) and Pucker Up Punch (see page 103) recipes.

2 cups coconut sugar

1 cup filtered water

2 vanilla beans, split lengthwise

One 1-pint Mason jar

Combine the coconut sugar and water in a medium pot over medium-high heat and bring to a boil. Continue to boil, stirring constantly, for 5 minutes, until the sugar has completely dissolved. Remove from the heat.

Place the vanilla beans in a Mason jar and pour the hot syrup over it. Set aside to steep for 8 hours. Ensure the seal is airtight, and store in the refrigerator.

Vanilla Syrup will keep in the refrigerator sealed in an airtight Mason jar for 1 month.

Magnesium, calcium and potassium are all components that make up the vanilla bean, and these minerals have superb benefits for your beautiful bod. It was considered an aphrodisiac by the ancient Mayans!

Watermelon *Syrup* MAKES APPROXIMATELY 1¼ CUPS

This delicious syrup, derived from the staple of all summer fruits, has an unmistakable flavor that's sweetened naturally, without the need for added refined sugar. Use this syrup in the Melonade (see page 167) recipe or drizzle it over your favorite fruit salad. You'll thank us!

½ cup coconut sugar

¼ cup filtered water

2 tablespoons chopped fresh mint leaves

1½ pounds diced fresh watermelon, pureed

2 tablespoons freshly squeezed lemon juice

One 1-pint Mason jar

Combine the coconut sugar, water, and mint leaves in a medium pot over medium-high heat and bring to a boil. Continue to boil, stirring constantly, until the sugar has completely dissolved. Remove from the heat, remove and discard the mint leaves, and set aside for 30 minutes to allow the syrup to steep.

Place the pureed watermelon in a mixing bowl and strain the cooled syrup into the bowl. Stir in the lemon juice.

Transfer the syrup to the Mason jar, ensure the seal is airtight, and store in the refrigerator.

> Watermelon Syrup will keep in the refrigerator sealed in an airtight Mason jar for 1 week.
>
> Each juicy piece of watermelon has substantial amounts of vitamin C, citrulline, and lycopene. Vitamin C also plays a role in healing, a trait that comes in handy should you stumble after drinking too many glasses of In Too Deep (see page 90).

Natural Sour *Mix* MAKES APPROXIMATELY 2 CUPS

Our clean Natural Sour Mix creates completely different cocktails than those made with the bright yellow, chemical-laden mixes you'll find on the shelves of your local store. It's extremely easy to make, and so versatile. The underlying citrus component provides an excellent source of vitamins C and B6, potassium, folate, and flavonoids. Try this sour mix in the Dr. Feel Good (see page 115) and Malibu Sour (see page 116) recipes.

¾ cup warm (not boiling) filtered water

½ cup freshly squeezed lemon juice

½ cup freshly squeezed lime juice

½ cup honey or coconut sugar

One 1-quart Mason jar

Whisk all of the ingredients together in a pitcher until the honey or coconut sugar is completely dissolved.

Strain the mix through cheesecloth and discard any solids. Transfer the mix to the Mason jar, ensure the seal is airtight, and store in the refrigerator.

> Natural Sour Mix will keep in the refrigerator sealed in an airtight Mason jar for 2 to 3 months.

BETTER BITTERS

Who said being bitter is a bad thing? Bitters, a combination of botanicals, aromatic herbs, and spices infused with clean spirits, have a long history as a digestive aid and as additives to drinks and cocktails. In fact, in the beginning, bitters were used solely for medicinal purposes, and their reputation as a flavoring agent developed over time. The bitter truth: Combining your own flavors is truly where the party starts.

Bitters include barks and leaves, each with its own flavor and scent. The flavors in our bitters come from ingredients like dandelion root, coriander seeds, fennel seeds, quassia bark, and wild cherry bark.

Aromatic or flavoring agents used include spices, flowers, and herbs; our recipes include star anise, cinnamon, citrus peel, lavender, and cacao beans. In order to maximize the flavor extracted from the agents, we recommend a neutral flavor base, such as vodka.

Don't forget to label all the jars once you are done to differentiate between the recipes—unlike the syrups, bitters can be difficult to tell apart. Due to their high alcohol content, bitters will last and last, although their flavors may mellow over time. You can hang on to your bitters for as long as they keep their aroma. These are high-volume recipes, but a bottle of homemade bitters makes a great gift.

Citrus *Bitters*

Citrus adds pizzazz to any cocktail and offers immunity-boosting and detoxification properties. Lemons and oranges are packed with vitamin C and also offer pectin, which fends off spikes in blood-sugar levels, and antioxidants, which stave off morning-after bloat. Vodka and gin cocktails pair well with this splash of brightness.

Freshly grated zest of 4 organic oranges*

Freshly grated zest of 2 organic Meyer lemons*

Two 1-quart Mason jars

One 750-ml bottle vodka

1 tablespoon fennel seeds

1 cinnamon stick

1/2 teaspoon whole cloves

1/2 teaspoon coriander seeds

Six 4-ounce brown glass dropper bottles

*Always rinse and dry citrus fruits before zesting.

Place the orange and lemon zest in one of the Mason jars and top with the remaining ingredients. Tightly seal the jar and store in a cool, dark place for 4 weeks, shaking the jar vigorously 4 times a week.

Pour the bitters through a fine mesh strainer into the remaining Mason jar and discard the solid contents of the strainer. Transfer the bitters to the 4-ounce brown glass dropper bottles and store, tightly sealed, at room temperature.

Floral *Bitters*

MAKES ABOUT SIX 4-OUNCE BROWN GLASS DROPPER BOTTLES

The addition of floral essence to your cocktail brings unexpected flavor layers of lavender, rose, and sage. The health benefits of bitters are primarily related to digestion, but floral bitters in particular have the added bonus of helping maintain blood-sugar levels and balancing appetite.

One 750-ml bottle vodka

Peel of 2 grapefruits, cut into strips

Peel of 1 lemon , cut into strips

Peel of 1 orange, cut into strips

5 sage leaves

5 rose petals

3 fresh lavender sprigs

3 whole star anise pods

Two ½-gallon Mason jars

Honey to taste

Six 4-ounce brown glass dropper bottles

Combine all of the ingredients except the honey in one of the Mason jars. Tightly seal the jar and store in a cool, dark place for 4 weeks, shaking the jar vigorously 4 times a week.

Pour the bitters through 2 layers of cheesecloth into the remaining Mason jar and discard the solid contents of the cheesecloth.

Add the honey. Transfer the bitters to the 4-ounce brown glass dropper bottles and store, tightly sealed, at room temperature.

Grapefruit *Bitters*

MAKES ABOUT SIX 4-OUNCE BROWN GLASS DROPPER BOTTLES

A twist on the Citrus Bitters, our Grapefruit Bitters recipe combines the essence of dandelion root, grapefruit peel, and cilantro together into a single gold mine of flavor. Herbalists use dandelion root to support the function of the liver, but savvy ladies eat grapefruit to clear up acne and to alleviate symptoms of PMS, like water retention. Grapefruit peel, which is crammed with antioxidants, gives this bitters recipe a smooth finish. The cilantro marries the flavors and helps with the digestion process. These bitters are delicious with tequila, gin, or vodka.

One 750-ml bottle vodka

Peel of 3 large or 5 medium grapefruits, cut into strips

Peel of 4 lemons, cut into strips

3 tablespoons minced fresh ginger

2 tablespoons chopped dried mint leaves

2 tablespoons chopped fresh cilantro

1 tablespoon whole cloves

1 tablespoon dried dandelion root

1 tablespoon dried gentian root

Two ½-gallon Mason jars

Six 4-ounce brown glass dropper bottles

Combine all of the ingredients in one of the Mason jars. Tightly seal the jar and store in a cool, dark place for 3 weeks. Do not touch or shake the jar.

Pour the bitters through 2 layers of cheesecloth into the remaining Mason jar, reserving the solid contents of the cheesecloth.

Bring 1½ cups of water to a simmer in a medium saucepan over medium heat. Tie the cheesecloth into a bundle, add it to the pan, and remove from the heat. Allow the spiced water to cool and steep overnight.

Remove and discard the cheesecloth bundle. Transfer the spiced water to the Mason jar containing the bitters and store in a cool, dark place for 1 week.

Pour the bitters through 2 layers of cheesecloth until the bitters are clear. Transfer the bitters to the 4-ounce brown glass dropper bottles and store, tightly sealed, at room temperature.

Chapter Three

Classics
(with a Twist)

Cold *Fashioned* SERVES 1

Traditionally, the Old Fashioned was considered a medicinal drink that aided in digestion. Our Cold Fashioned adds iced coffee for a kick in energy and a boost in metabolism.

RECOMMENDED BARWARE

ROCKS GLASS

2 orange slices

2 ounces brewed coffee, cold

1 ounce bourbon

½ ounce Cinnamon Girl Syrup (see page 28)

Ice

Garnish: Orange twist

Muddle 1 of the orange slices in a cocktail shaker. Pour in the coffee, bourbon, and Cinnamon Girl Syrup and add the ice. Stir gently to chill the ingredients.

Strain the contents of the shaker into an ice-filled rocks glass. Garnish with an orange twist and serve.

My Drunk Aunt *Said So* SERVES 1

Just like our favorite drunk aunt always used to say, this combination of ginger, bourbon, and lemon is sure to cure the common cold. And it's one of our favorites.

RECOMMENDED BARWARE

COPPER MUG

½ cup brewed ginger tea, cold

½ tablespoon honey

1 ounce bourbon

1½ tablespoons freshly squeezed lemon juice

½ ounce maple syrup

Ice

Garnish: Ginger coins

Stir together the ginger tea and honey in a copper mug until well blended. Add the bourbon, lemon juice, and maple syrup and stir again until the maple syrup is dissolved.

Add the ice, garnish with ginger coins, and serve.

"Dated" *Old Fashioned* SERVES 1

This cocktail, while classic, need not be "dated" . . . especially when it's made with our unique and flavorful Date Syrup instead of a traditional simple syrup, which uses refined sugar.

RECOMMENDED BARWARE

ROCKS GLASS

One 2-inch orange peel piece, pith removed

2 ounces bourbon

1 ounce Date Syrup
(see page 30)

3 dashes Citrus Bitters
(see page 43)

Ice

Garnish: Orange wedge and
½ Medjool date

Muddle the orange peel in a cocktail shaker. Add the bourbon, Date Syrup, Citrus Bitters, and ice and shake for 10 seconds.

Strain the contents of the shaker into an ice-filled rocks glass. Garnish with an orange wedge and date half and serve.

Twisted SERVES 1

This modern twist on the Old Fashioned adds Vanilla Syrup for a smoother finish. The end result is a beautiful balance of sweetness and bitterness from the orange peels. This drink will make a bourbon lover out of even the harshest critic.

RECOMMENDED BARWARE

HIGHBALL GLASS

One 1-inch orange peel piece, pith removed

¼ teaspoon coconut sugar

¼ teaspoon filtered water

3 dashes Citrus Bitters (see page 43)

2 ounces bourbon

½ ounce Vanilla Syrup (see page 37)

Ice

Garnish: Orange wedge

Muddle the orange peel, sugar, and Citrus Bitters in a cocktail shaker. Add the water and continue muddling until all the sugar has dissolved. Add the bourbon, Vanilla Syrup, and ice to the shaker and stir softly.

Strain the contents of the shaker into an ice-filled highball glass. Garnish with an orange wedge and serve.

Very Berry Julep **SERVES 1**

This modern spin on a classic Southern cocktail is made with fresh raspberries and raspberry jam. This drink has been known to make a girl feel fancy . . . after all, this cocktail is a mainstay at the greatest American horse race, the Kentucky Derby.

RECOMMENDED BARWARE

COPPER MUG

4 to 6 fresh raspberries

8 to 10 fresh mint leaves

2 ounces bourbon

1½ teaspoons organic unsweetened raspberry jam

Ice

Garnish: Raspberries and mint leaves

Muddle all but one of the raspberries and most of the mint leaves in a cocktail shaker. Add the bourbon, raspberry jam, and ice and shake for 10 seconds. Check to ensure that the jam is completely dissolved.

Strain the contents of the shaker into an ice-filled copper mug. Garnish with the remaining raspberry and mint leaves and serve.

Prohibition SERVES 1

This is a more natural take on a popular Prohibition-era cocktail that used citrus and honey to mask the scent of gin. Fortunately, today's gin smells and tastes much better than the 1920s bathtub variety.

RECOMMENDED BARWARE

ROCKS GLASS

2 ounces gin

1 ounce freshly squeezed lemon juice

1 ounce freshly squeezed orange juice

¾ ounce Honey Syrup (see page 32)

3 dashes Citrus Bitters (see page 43)

Ice

Seltzer water

Garnish: Lemon and orange wedges and mint leaf

Combine the gin, lemon and orange juices, Honey Syrup, and Citrus Bitters in a rocks glass and stir gently. Add ice to the glass and top off with the seltzer.

Garnish with lemon and orange wedges and a mint leaf and serve.

Strawberry *Limeade* SERVES 1

This refreshing drink was inspired by our trips to the Jersey Shore with our kids. After a run to the organic farm, we would unload our fresh fruits and make limeade. For an adult-approved upgrade, we added gin to the mix for a tart midday cocktail reminiscent of a glass of lemonade but without all the sugar.

RECOMMENDED BARWARE

HIGHBALL GLASS

1 lime

Ice

2 fresh strawberries, thinly sliced

2 ounces gin

½ cup seltzer water

Garnish: Strawberry slice

Using a peeler or paring knife, remove 2 long, thin tendrils of the lime's zest, taking care not to remove any of the pith. Fill a highball glass with ice.

Twist the zest tendrils and press them into the ice-filled glass to release their oils. Add all but 1 of the strawberry slices and the gin to the glass and top off with the seltzer.

Garnish with the remaining strawberry slice and serve.

FOR A PITCHER (SERVES 6):

3 limes

Ice

1 pint fresh strawberries, thinly sliced

1½ cups gin

Seltzer water

Garnish: Strawberry slices

Using a peeler, remove 6 long, thin tendrils of the limes' zest, taking care not to remove any of the pith. Fill 6 highball glasses with ice.

Twist the zest tendrils and press them into the ice-filled glasses to release their oils. Slightly muddle all but 6 of the strawberry slices in a pitcher and add the gin. Pour the contents of the pitcher into 6 highball glasses and top off each with the seltzer.

Garnish each with the remaining strawberry slices and serve.

The Doctor Is Out SERVES 1

Our grandmas always told us that a hot toddy will cure the common cold. Unlike the classic toddy recipe, we recommend replacing traditional bourbon with a taste of the unexpected—gin—the next time you're sick and the doctor is out.

RECOMMENDED BARWARE

COPPER MUG

2 ounces gin

1 ounce freshly squeezed lemon juice

1 ounce hot filtered water

½ ounce Honey Syrup (see page 32), warmed

2 dashes Citrus Bitters (see page 43)

Garnish: Lemon wheel

Combine the gin, lemon juice, hot water, Honey Syrup, and Citrus Bitters in a copper mug and stir until well combined.

Garnish with a lemon wheel and serve.

Violet Beauregard **SERVES 1**

This cocktail has all the attitude of a competitive gum-snapping tween and all the flavor of a giant, exploding blueberry. We usually serve this over ice in a larger glass, but if you want to fancy it up for company, you can strain it into coupe glasses.

RECOMMENDED BARWARE

ROCKS GLASS OR MASON JAR

½ cup fresh mint leaves

⅓ cup organic unsweetened blueberry juice

2 ounces gin

½ ounce freshly squeezed lime juice

1 tablespoon pure maple syrup

Ice

½ cup seltzer water

Garnish: Blueberries, mint leaves, or lime wheel

Muddle most of the mint leaves in a cocktail shaker. Add the blueberry juice, gin, lime juice, maple syrup, and ice and shake well for 10 seconds. Strain the contents of the shaker into an ice-filled rocks glass or Mason jar and top off with the seltzer.

Garnish with blueberries and the remaining mint leaves or lime wheel and serve.

Basilrita SERVES 1

A basil margarita stripped down to only the essentials . . . sometimes, you just shouldn't mess with perfection.

RECOMMENDED BARWARE

ROCKS GLASS

2 ounces silver tequila

½ ounce Basil Syrup (see page 27)

4 dashes Floral Bitters (see page 44)

Ice

Garnish: Basil leaves

Combine all of the ingredients except the basil leaves in an ice-filled rocks glass and stir until well combined.

Garnish with basil leaves and serve.

The Lusty Martini SERVES 1

Your guests will love this après-dinner cocktail. The mood-enhancing compounds found in cacao trigger the release of endorphins that are much like the ones generated when we're feeling amorous. Let's just say that the Lusty Martini may lead to an interesting evening.

RECOMMENDED BARWARE

MARTINI GLASS

3 to 4 tablespoons raw cacao powder

Pinch of sea salt

2 orange wedges

2 ounces brewed coffee, cold

2 ounces vodka

1 ounce light coconut milk

½ ounce maple syrup

½ teaspoon vanilla extract

Ice

Garnish: Coffee beans and orange wedge

Combine the cacao powder and salt on a plate or in a wide, shallow bowl. Rim a martini glass with 1 of the orange wedges and dip the rim of the glass into the cacao powder/salt mixture. Set aside.

Combine the coffee, vodka, coconut milk, maple syrup, vanilla extract, and ice in a cocktail shaker and shake for 10 seconds, until bubbly.

Strain the contents of the shaker into the prepared martini glass, garnish with coffee beans and the remaining orange wedge, and serve.

The Odd Couple SERVES 6

Like Felix and Oscar, watermelon and bourbon may appear mismatched, but they make for a pretty great team and ensure an evening of nonstop laughter. Think of this as a healthier version of a Manhattan.

RECOMMENDED BARWARE

MARGARITA GLASSES AND A PITCHER

4 cups frozen diced watermelon

2 cups coconut water

3 cups diced fresh pineapple

1 to 1¼ cups organic bourbon

1 cup fresh mint leaves

½ cup freshly squeezed lemon juice

1 tablespoon cherry juice

4 cups ice

Garnish: Lemon wedges and small watermelon wedges

Combine all of the ingredients except the lemon and watermelon wedges in a powerful blender and puree until smooth.

Pour the contents of the blender into 6 margarita glasses. Garnish each with lemon and watermelon wedges and serve.

FOR A SINGLE DRINK

½ cup frozen diced watermelon

½ cup coconut water

¼ cup diced fresh pineapple

¼ cup fresh mint leaves

1 to 2 ounces bourbon

1 ounce freshly squeezed lemon juice

1 teaspoon cherry juice

1 cup ice

Garnish: Lemon wedge and small watermelon wedge

Combine all of the ingredients except the lemon and watermelon wedges in a powerful blender and puree until smooth.

Pour the contents of the blender into a rocks glass, garnish with lemon and watermelon wedges, and serve.

Coconut-Cucumber *Margarita* SERVES 6

A clean and refreshing take on the very popular classic margarita, this coconut-cucumber mixture will make you yearn for warm and sunny days. Make a pitcher for your friends, because this cocktail is a real crowd pleaser.

RECOMMENDED BARWARE

ROCKS GLASSES AND A PITCHER

Sea salt

6 lime wedges

Ice

2 medium cucumbers, peeled (will yield 1 to 2 cups cucumber puree) *x3 = 6*

1½ cups silver tequila

½ cup freshly squeezed lemon juice *x 1.5 cups*

½ cup freshly squeezed lime juice *x 1.5 cups*

¼ to ½ cup Coconut Syrup (see page 29) *.75 cups*

Garnish: Lime wedges, cucumber spears, rosemary sprigs (optional)

Scatter the salt on a plate or in a wide, shallow bowl. Rim 6 margarita glasses with 1 of the lime wedges and dip the rim of each glass into the salt. Fill each glass with ice and set aside.

Place the cucumbers in a powerful blender and puree until smooth. Strain the contents of the blender through a fine mesh strainer.

Combine the strained cucumber puree, tequila, lemon and lime juices, and Coconut Syrup in a pitcher and stir until well combined. Strain the contents of the pitcher into the prepared glasses, garnish each with the remaining lime wedges, cucumber spears, and rosemary (if using), and serve.

FOR A SINGLE DRINK

Sea salt

2 lime wedges

Ice

2 ounces strained cucumber puree

2 ounces silver tequila

½ ounce freshly squeezed
lemon juice

½ ounce freshly squeezed
lime juice

½ ounce Coconut Syrup
(see page 29)

Garnish: Lime wedge and
cucumber spear (optional)

Using the salt and 1 of the lime wedges, rim a
margarita glass as stated above.

Prepare the cucumber puree as stated above.

Combine the cucumber puree, silver tequila, lemon
and lime juices, and Coconut Syrup in a cocktail
glass. Add the ice and stir for 10 seconds. Pour the
contents of the cocktail glass into the prepared
margarita glass. Garnish with the remaining lime
wedge and cucumber spear, if using, and serve.

Cooling Cucumber *Mojito* SERVES 1

This cocktail is perfect for a hot summer night. Cucumbers, which are made up of almost 95 percent water, are a great way to cool the body and keep you hydrated. Cucumbers are also really low in calories, which makes this drink relatively guilt free and allows you to pair it with some naughty chips and guacamole.

RECOMMENDED BARWARE

ROCKS GLASS

Sea salt

1 lime wedge

One 3-inch piece peeled cucumber

¼ cup fresh mint leaves, torn in half

2 ounces freshly squeezed lime juice

2 ounces silver tequila

1 ounce Honey Syrup (see page 32)

Ice

Seltzer water

Garnish: Cucumber slice and mint leaves

Scatter the salt on a plate or in a wide, shallow bowl. Rim a rocks glass with the lime wedge and dip the rim of the glass into the salt.

Place the 3-inch cucumber piece in a powerful blender and puree until smooth. Strain the contents of the blender through a fine mesh strainer.

Combine most of the mint leaves, the lime juice, the tequila, the strained cucumber puree, and the Honey Syrup in a cocktail shaker. Add the ice and shake for 10 seconds.

Strain the contents of the shaker an ice-filled rocks glass and top off with the seltzer. Garnish with a cucumber slice and the remaining mint leaves and serve.

Sweet Basil *Gimlet* SERVES 1

Sip on one of these after a rough day at the office. Basil is a powerful adaptogen that helps your body respond to stress, and the bitters in the drink can help calm an upset stomach.

RECOMMENDED BARWARE

ROCKS GLASS

5 slices cucumber

5 fresh basil leaves

2 ounces vodka

1 ounce freshly squeezed lemon juice

½ ounce Basil Syrup (see page 27)

3 dashes Citrus Bitters (see page 43)

Ice

Seltzer water

Garnish: Basil leaf

Muddle the cucumber and all but 1 of the basil leaves in a cocktail shaker. Add the vodka, lemon juice, Basil Syrup, Citrus Bitters, and ice and shake vigorously.

Strain the contents of the shaker into an ice-filled rocks glass and top off with the seltzer. Garnish with the remaining basil leaf and serve.

Mad Tea *Party* SERVES 1

The Mad Tea Party is a healthier twist on the Long Island Iced Tea. After all, no one is really sure what goes into a traditional Long Island Iced Tea, but we guarantee you won't find any tea in it. We like this over ice but it can be fun to strain and serve in a martini glass, as pictured.

RECOMMENDED BARWARE

HIGHBALL GLASS

2 ounces brewed black or green tea, cold

1 ounce Honey Syrup (see page 32)

1 ounce freshly squeezed lemon juice

½ ounce gin

½ ounce silver tequila

½ ounce vodka

3 dashes Citrus Bitters (see page 43)

Ice

Garnish: Lemon twist

Combine the tea, Honey Syrup, lemon juice, gin, tequila, vodka, and Citrus Bitters in a highball glass and stir until well combined.

Add the ice to the glass, garnish with a lemon twist, and serve.

Chapter Four

Sweet *and* Fruity

Blackberry *Crush* SERVES 1

We love the tart flavor of blackberries, but we don't love it when their seeds get stuck in our teeth. That's where the strainer comes in handy! The sweet zing of the blackberries works beautifully with the citrus juices and a hint of rosemary, making this a light and refreshing drink.

RECOMMENDED BARWARE

ROCKS GLASS

¼ cup fresh blackberries

1 ounce vodka or gin

½ ounce freshly squeezed lemon juice

½ ounce freshly squeezed lime juice

1 tablespoon Honey Syrup (see page 32)

Ice

Seltzer water

Garnish: Rosemary sprig and blackberries

Muddle most of the blackberries in a cocktail shaker. Add the vodka, lemon and lime juices, Honey Syrup, and ice and shake for 10 seconds.

Strain the contents of the shaker into an ice-filled rocks glass and top off with the seltzer. Garnish with a rosemary sprig and the remaining blackberries and serve.

Three-Tequila-Floor *Sangria* SERVES 6 TO 8

This cocktail can go down a little too fast because of its sweet flavors. You'll want to sip this one slowly, or you won't know what hit you (hint . . . it's very likely the floor).

RECOMMENDED BARWARE

HIGHBALL GLASSES

2 cups silver tequila

One 16-ounce can coconut water

2 cups frozen strawberries

1 cup frozen peaches

1 cup filtered water, if needed

¼ cup Coconut Syrup
(see page 29)

2 fresh cilantro sprigs

Seltzer water

Garnish: Fresh strawberries or
fresh sliced peaches

Combine the tequila, coconut water, frozen strawberries, frozen peaches, water (if needed), Coconut Syrup, and cilantro sprigs in a powerful blender and process until slushy.

Pour the contents of the blender into 6 to 8 highball glasses. Top off each glass with the seltzer, garnish each with fresh strawberries or peaches, and serve.

Berry Berry *Rosemary* SERVES 1

Blackberries have a higher concentration of antioxidants than any other fruit. This drink, which combines the blackberries with the anti-inflammatory and antiseptic properties of rosemary, can improve your mental energy and help you concentrate during your next late-night poker game.

RECOMMENDED BARWARE

MASON JAR

½ cup fresh blackberries

2 orange slices

3 fresh rosemary sprigs

1 teaspoon coconut sugar

2 ounces gin

Ice

Seltzer water

Garnish: Rosemary sprig and blackberry

Muddle all but 1 of the blackberries, the orange slices, 2 of the rosemary sprigs, and the coconut sugar in a cocktail shaker. Add the gin and ice and shake for 10 seconds.

Strain the contents of the shaker into a Mason jar filled with ice and top off with the seltzer. Garnish with the remaining rosemary sprig and blackberry and serve.

Fresh BeGINings   SERVES 1

The marriage of kale and sweet pineapple is the basis of Fresh BeGINings. Both are high in magnesium and other vital compounds that promote anti-aging. Basil rounds out this powerhouse by adding its share of adaptogens, which help us deal with the stress life throws at us.

RECOMMENDED BARWARE

HIGHBALL GLASS

¼ cup fresh pineapple wedges

3 fresh basil leaves, chopped

½ cup organic kale juice

2 ounces gin or vodka

Ice

Garnish: Pineapple wedge

Muddle all but 1 of the pineapple wedges and the basil leaves in a cocktail shaker until there are no large pieces remaining. Add the kale juice, gin, and ice and shake for 10 seconds.

Strain the contents of the shaker into an ice-filled highball glass, garnish with the remaining pineapple wedge, and serve.

The Fertile Blonde SERVES 1

It's no surprise that pineapple is loaded with immunity-boosting vitamin C, which is known to prevent premature aging and damage from free radicals. But did you know that the vitamins, minerals, and nutrients in pineapple can boost fertility in both women and men? Please take this under advisement.

RECOMMENDED BARWARE

MARTINI GLASS

2 orange wedges

½ cup toasted shredded coconut

½ cup cubed pineapple

¼ cup freshly squeezed orange juice

½ ounce Coconut Syrup (see page 29)

2 ounces gin

Ice

Garnish: **Orange wedge and shredded coconut**

Scatter most of the shredded coconut on a plate or in a wide, shallow bowl. Rim a martini glass with 1 of the orange wedges and dip the rim of the glass into the coconut. Set aside.

Muddle the pineapple, orange juice, and Coconut Syrup in a cocktail shaker. Add the gin and ice and shake for 10 seconds.

Strain the contents of the shaker into the prepared glass. Garnish with the remaining orange wedge and shredded coconut and serve.

> To toast coconut: Preheat the oven to 325°F. Evenly scatter shredded or flaked coconut on a large baking sheet lined with parchment paper. Bake for 4 minutes, stir, and bake for 3 more minutes. Keep an eye on it, as once it starts to turn golden, it goes quickly.

SuBourbon *Problems* SERVES 6

Do your neighbors leave their barking dog outside all day long just to torment the neighborhood? Welcome to suburbia. Combat this mundane suburban BS with the not-so-mundane SuBourbon Problems. Make nice with your neighbors and invite them in for a cocktail as well.

RECOMMENDED BARWARE

**CHILLED MARTINI GLASSES
AND A PITCHER**

2 cups fresh raspberries

1½ cups chopped fresh basil leaves

¼ cup plus 1 tablespoon coconut sugar

1 cup bourbon

Freshly squeezed juice of 5 to 6 fresh limes

Ice

Seltzer water

Garnish: Raspberries, lime wedges, and basil leaves

Combine all but 6 of the raspberries, most of the basil leaves, and the coconut sugar in a saucepan over medium heat and cook, stirring constantly, for 5 to 7 minutes, until the sugar dissolves and the raspberries start to break down. Remove from the heat and set aside to cool.

Combine the raspberry mixture, bourbon, lime juice, and ice in a pitcher and stir until well combined. Strain the contents of the pitcher into 6 chilled martini glasses and top off each with the seltzer.

Garnish each with the remaining raspberries, lime wedges, and basil leaves and serve.

In Too *Deep* SERVES 6

Watermelon is great for hydration and is rich in citrulline, an enzyme that promotes blood flow throughout the body and is great for libido. Clearly, we should all eat more watermelon.

RECOMMENDED BARWARE

MARGARITA GLASSES

1¼ cups silver tequila

1¼ cups watermelon juice

3 cups ice

Garnish: Mint leaves and freshly grated orange zest

Combine the tequila, watermelon juice, and ice in a powerful blender and process until slushy.

Pour the contents of the blender into 6 margarita glasses, garnish each with mint leaves and orange zest, and serve.

The Pie Shooter   SERVES 5

This drink offers all of the delicious flavors of a coconut cream pie in one yummy shot, with the added benefits of vitamins B complex and C.

RECOMMENDED BARWARE

2-OUNCE SHOT GLASSES

Toasted coconut flakes
(see page 86)

2 lime wedges

½ cup silver tequila

3 ounces coconut water

Freshly squeezed juice of 1 lime

1 ounce Coconut Syrup
(see page 29)

Ice

Garnish: Lime wheels and
shredded coconut

Scatter the toasted shredded coconut on a plate or in a wide, shallow bowl. Rim 5 shot glasses with the lime wedges and dip the rims of the glasses into the coconut. Set aside.

Combine the tequila, coconut water, lime juice, Coconut Syrup, and ice in a cocktail shaker and shake for 10 seconds.

Strain the contents of the shaker into the prepared shot glasses, garnish with lime wheels and shredded coconut, and serve.

SweetTart SERVES 1

Just like your favorite candy from when you were a kid, this cocktail offers a variety of sweet and sour flavors wrapped up in a cute package!

RECOMMENDED BARWARE

HIGHBALL GLASS

2 ounces silver tequila

¾ ounce freshly squeezed lime juice

¾ ounce organic unsweetened tart cherry juice

2 dashes Citrus Bitters (see page 43)

Ice

Seltzer water

Garnish: Pomegranate seeds and lime wedge

Combine the tequila, lime juice, cherry juice, Citrus Bitters, and ice in a cocktail shaker and shake for 10 seconds.

Strain the contents of the shaker into an ice-filled highball glass and top off with the seltzer. Garnish with pomegranate seeds and lime wedge and serve.

Pineapple *Fizz* SERVES 1

This sparkling punch tastes just as good as it looks. Limes contain compounds with antioxidant benefits, and pineapple provides copper and essential minerals that reduce inflammation. As an added bonus, the natural sugars in pineapple offer a much healthier alternative to refined sweeteners.

RECOMMENDED BARWARE

HIGHBALL GLASS

8 to 10 fresh basil leaves

½ ounce freshly squeezed lime juice

¼ cup pineapple juice

2 ounces vodka

Ice

Seltzer water

Garnish: Pineapple slice and basil leaf

Muddle all but 1 of the basil leaves and the lime juice in a cocktail shaker. Add the pineapple juice, vodka, and ice and shake for 10 seconds.

Strain the contents of the shaker into an ice-filled highball glass and top off with the seltzer. Garnish with a pineapple slice and the remaining basil leaf and serve.

We're *Jammin'* SERVES 1

This cocktail makes us wax nostalgic for our college days, when we'd sit on the front porch drinking cocktails with Bob Marley echoing throughout the house.

RECOMMENDED BARWARE

MASON JAR

2 ounces gin

2 ounces vodka

2 ounces freshly squeezed lemon juice

½ ounce Honey Syrup (see page 32)

1 teaspoon organic berry preserves

Ice

Seltzer water

Garnish: Berries and mint sprig

Combine the gin, vodka, lemon juice, Honey Syrup, and berry preserves in an 8-ounce Mason jar. Add the ice and tightly cover with the lid.

Shake the jar until the jam is thoroughly incorporated into the liquid. Remove the lid and top off with the seltzer. Garnish with the berries and a mint sprig and serve.

In the Mood *for a* Melony Martini

SERVES 1

Cantaloupe is an excellent source of immunity-boosting vitamin C as well as omega-3 fatty acids, which combat the moody blues. This drink will make you dance and sing.

RECOMMENDED BARWARE

MARTINI GLASS

Four 2-ounce cantaloupe chunks, blended and strained

2 fresh basil sprigs

2 ounces vodka

½ ounce Ginger Syrup (see page 31)

¼ ounce Basil Syrup (see page 27)

Ice

Garnish: Canteloupe ball and basil leaf

Muddle the cantaloupe puree and 1 of the basil sprigs in a cocktail shaker. Add the vodka, Ginger Syrup, Basil Syrup, and ice and shake for 10 seconds.

Strain the contents of the shaker into a martini glass. Garnish with a canteloupe ball and the remaining basil sprig and serve.

My Darling *Clementine* SERVES 1

It's a flavor we don't often use, as these little cuties are only in season from November to January. Slightly sweeter than oranges, clementines can make perfect cocktails for your holiday dinner party.

RECOMMENDED BARWARE

ROCKS GLASS

2 ounces freshly squeezed clementine juice

2 ounces unsweetened cranberry juice

1½ ounces vodka

Ice

Seltzer water

Garnish: Clementine wedge

Combine the clementine juice, cranberry juice, and vodka in a cocktail shaker filled with ice and shake for 10 seconds.

Strain the contents of the shaker into an ice-filled rocks glass. Top off with the seltzer, garnish with a clementine wedge, and serve.

Pucker Up *Punch* SERVES 1

If you love lemons like we do, you'll enjoy this tart cocktail. Lemons are packed full of vitamin C, and raspberries are loaded with vitamin K and magnesium, which protect you from free radicals and promote bone health.

RECOMMENDED BARWARE

COUPETTE OR MARTINI GLASS

½ cup fresh raspberries

1 ounce freshly squeezed lemon juice

¾ ounce Vanilla Syrup (see page 37)

2 ounces vodka

3 to 5 dashes Citrus Bitters (see page 43)

Ice

Garnish: Raspberry and lemon twist

Muddle all but 1 of the raspberries, the lemon juice, and the Vanilla Syrup in a cocktail shaker, making sure to release all of the raspberries' juices. Add the vodka, Citrus Bitters, and ice and shake for 10 seconds.

Strain the contents of the shaker into a coupette or martini glass, garnish with the remaining raspberry and a lemon twist, and serve.

Chapter Five

Tart *and* Spicy

The Day Drinker   SERVES 6

This cocktail is sunshine in a glass. Loaded with the strong antioxidant vitamin C, we like to think of the Day Drinker as the perfect immunity booster when typhoid hits your house. You could tote this one to t-ball games, but bring enough for your friends . . . sports moms always covet!

RECOMMENDED BARWARE

ROCKS GLASSES AND A PITCHER

3 lemons, cut into quarters

12 fresh sage leaves, torn in half

3 teaspoons coconut sugar

1½ cups gin

1½ cups freshly squeezed grapefruit juice

Ice

Garnish: Sage leaves and grapefruit wheels

Muddle the lemons, one-half of the sage leaves, and the coconut sugar in a pitcher. Add the gin, grapefruit juice, and ice and stir until well combined.

Strain the contents of the pitcher into 6 ice-filled rocks glasses. Garnish each with the remaining sage leaves and grapefruit wheels and serve.

FOR A SINGLE DRINK

¼ lemon

3 fresh sage leaves, torn in half

½ teaspoon coconut sugar

2 ounces gin

2 ounces freshly squeezed grapefruit juice

Ice

Garnish: Sage leaf and grapefruit wheel

Muddle the lemon quarter, 2 of the sage leaves, and coconut sugar in a cocktail shaker. Add the gin and grapefruit juice and shake for 10 seconds.

Strain the contents of the shaker into an ice-filled rocks glass, garnish with the remaining sage leaf and a grapefruit wheel, and serve.

Beast *of* Bourbon

Trust us when we say that bourbon brings out the beast in all of us. As Mick Jagger sings, "Let's go home and draw the curtains/Music on the radio . . . ." We definitely recommend adding this smooth cocktail to the scenario.

RECOMMENDED BARWARE

COUPETTE OR MARTINI GLASS

½ cup fresh blackberries

½ lemon, cut into slices

2 ounces freshly squeezed lemon juice

2 ounces bourbon

½ ounce Coconut Syrup (see page 29)

Ice

Garnish: Blackberry and lemon slice

Muddle all but 1 of the blackberries, all but 1 of the lemon slices, Coconut Syrup, and the lemon juice in a cocktail shaker. Add the bourbon and ice and shake for 10 seconds.

Strain the contents of the shaker into a coupette or martini glass, garnish with the remaining blackberry and lemon slice, and serve.

The 5-Minute Warning SERVES 4 TO 6

Many of us have issued a 5-minute warning, an advance notice designed to avoid a public meltdown of gargantuan proportions when pulling a child (or partner, or spouse) away from an enjoyable activity. The deliciously light and joyful flavors of this cocktail should take the edge off when the meltdown ensues anyway.

RECOMMENDED BARWARE

ROCKS GLASSES AND A PITCHER

3 fresh limes, cut into wedges

1 bunch fresh mint leaves

1½ jalapeño peppers, seeded and diced

4 cups fresh frozen watermelon chunks, pureed

1 cup silver tequila

Ice

Seltzer water

Muddle the lime wedges, mint leaves, and jalapeño peppers in a pitcher. Stir in the pureed watermelon and tequila.

Strain the contents of the pitcher into 6 ice-filled rocks glasses, top off each with the seltzer, and serve.

FOR A SINGLE DRINK

¼ cup fresh mint leaves

1 ounce freshly squeezed lime juice

½ jalapeño pepper, seeded and diced

¼ cup frozen watermelon chunks, pureed

2 ounces tequila

Seltzer water

Muddle the mint leaves, lime juice, and jalapeño pepper in a cocktail shaker. Add the pureed watermelon and tequila and shake vigorously.

Strain the contents of the shaker into an ice-filled rocks glass, top off with the seltzer, and serve.

The Perfect Storm **SERVES 1**

This cocktail's combination of bold tequila and the intense flavors of ginger and Citrus Bitters make it a "swell" choice when the weather turns.

RECOMMENDED BARWARE

ROCKS GLASS

2 ounces silver tequila

1 ounce freshly squeezed lemon juice

¾ ounce Ginger Syrup (see page 31)

3 dashes Citrus Bitters (see page 43)

Ice

Seltzer water

Garnish: Lemon wedge and mint leaf

Combine the tequila, lemon juice, Ginger Syrup, Citrus Bitters, and ice in a cocktail shaker and shake for 10 seconds.

Strain the contents of the shaker into an ice-filled rocks glass and top off with the seltzer. Garnish with a lemon wedge and mint leaf and serve.

One Hot *Matcha* SERVES 1

In this cocktail, a touch of Jalapeño Syrup pairs unexpectedly with the earthy bitterness of green tea and bourbon—making this one hot matcha.

RECOMMENDED BARWARE

COUPETTE OR MARTINI GLASS

½ ounce Matcha Tea Syrup
(see page 35)

¼ teaspoon Jalapeño Syrup
(see page 34)

½ teaspoon filtered water

2 ounces bourbon

Garnish: Jalapeño pepper slice

Combine the Matcha Tea Syrup, Jalapeño Syrup, and water in a cocktail shaker. Add the bourbon and ice and shake.

Pour the contents of the cocktail shaker into a coupette or martini glass, garnish with a jalapeño pepper slice, and serve.

Matcha is a special type of powdered green tea that's grown and ground in Japan. The tea bushes are put in the shade for the last three weeks of their growth, increasing their chlorophyll content and deepening their green color. Matcha's unique characteristic is that it energizes you without adding the typical caffeine crazies.

Dr. Feel *Good* SERVES 1

The antioxidants in cranberries are widely known for their ability to alleviate symptoms of infections, sore throats, and common colds. We aren't suggesting you ignore your symptoms. Instead, we highly recommend paying a visit to Dr. Feel Good! He's the one who "makes ya feel alright."

RECOMMENDED BARWARE

COUPETTE OR MARTINI GLASS

2 ounces bourbon

2 ounces unsweetened cranberry juice

1/2 ounce Coconut Syrup (see page 29)

1/2 ounce Natural Sour Mix (see page 39)

Ice

Garnish: Cranberry and lime wheel

Combine the bourbon, cranberry juice, Coconut Syrup, and Natural Sour Mix in an ice-filled rocks glass and stir until well combined.

Garnish with a cranberry and lime wheel and serve.

Malibu *Sour* SERVES 1

Whether all the leaves are brown or the sky is grey, this Malibu Sour has us California dreamin', even on a winter's day.

RECOMMENDED BARWARE

HIGHBALL GLASS

1 lime wedge

Sea salt

Ice

2 ounces silver tequila

1 ounce Coconut Syrup
(see page 29)

1 ounce freshly squeezed
grapefruit juice

½ ounce freshly squeezed
lime juice

½ ounce Natural Sour Mix
(see page 39)

Garnish: Slender grapefruit
wedge or lime wheel

Scatter the salt on a plate or in a wide, shallow bowl. Rim a highball glass with the lime wedge and dip the rim of the glass into the salt. Fill the glass with ice and set aside.

Combine the tequila, grapefruit and lime juices, Coconut Syrup, Natural Sour Mix, and ice in a cocktail shaker and shake for 10 seconds.

Strain the contents of the shaker into the prepared glass, garnish with a grapefruit wedge or lime wheel, and serve.

The Liquid Muscle Relaxer **SERVES 1**

This drink offers a double shot of anti-inflammatories that can help reduce muscle pain. In fact, ginger is considered to be a natural remedy for those who cannot tolerate ibuprofen or aspirin.

RECOMMENDED BARWARE

HIGHBALL GLASS

1 lemon, quartered

2 tablespoons freshly grated ginger

2 ounces vodka

1 teaspoon Ginger Syrup (see page 31)

Ice

1 tablespoon freshly grated turmeric (optional)

Seltzer water

Garnish: Ginger coin and lemon quarters

Muddle 2 of the lemon quarters and the grated ginger in a cocktail shaker. Add the vodka, Ginger Syrup, ice, and turmeric, if using, and shake for 10 seconds.

Strain the contents of the shaker into an ice-filled highball glass and top off with the seltzer. Garnish with a ginger coin and the remaining lemon quarters and serve.

Your Latin *Lover* SERVES 1

We love tart and spicy, and this cocktail hits all the right notes. Grapefruit and jalapeño peppers together? It shouldn't be this good, but OH MY, is it ever! Make a pitcher of it and salsa the night away.

RECOMMENDED BARWARE

HIGHBALL GLASS

2 ounces silver tequila *(40 oz)*

2 ounces freshly squeezed grapefruit juice *(6 oz)*

Freshly squeezed juice of 1 medium to large lime *(12oz)*

1 ounce Jalapeño Syrup (see page 34) *(12oz)*

Ice

Seltzer water

Garnish: Jalapeño pepper slice and lime wheel

Combine the tequila, grapefruit and lime juices, Jalapeño Syrup, and ice in a highball glass and stir.

Top off with the seltzer, garnish with a jalapeño slice and lime wheel, and serve.

The Kiss SERVES 1

Pomegranates are loaded with polyphenolic flavonoids that are as antibacterial as prescription mouthwash, so sip on one of these and lean in.

RECOMMENDED BARWARE

ROCKS GLASS

2 ounces silver tequila

1 ounce freshly squeezed lime juice

½ ounce pomegranate juice

½ ounce Jalapeño Syrup (see page 34)

Ice

Garnish: Pomegranate seeds and lime wedge

Combine the tequila, lime and pomegranate juices, Jalapeño Syrup, and ice in a cocktail shaker and shake for 10 seconds.

Pour the contents of the shaker into an ice-filled rocks glass. Garnish with pomegranate seeds and a lime wedge and serve.

eyer *Lemonade* SERVES 6 TO 8

Meyer lemons are a cross between a regular lemon and a mandarin orange. The sweet and sour flavors make this drink go down easy.

RECOMMENDED BARWARE

MASON JARS AND A PITCHER

[handwritten: 4 cups per quart   3 quarts ×]

[handwritten: 1 cup = 8 oz]

2½ to 3 cups vodka

2 cups freshly squeezed Meyer lemon juice *[handwritten: → 16 oz]* (or regular lemons if you can't find Meyer)

1½ to 2 cup Honey Syrup *[handwritten: → 16 oz]* (see page 32)

Zest of 6 Meyer lemons

Garnish: Lemon wheels

Combine the vodka, lemon juice, Honey Syrup, and lemon zest in a pitcher and stir until combined.

Pour the contents of the pitcher into 6 ice-filled Mason jars, garnish each with lemon wheels, and serve.

[handwritten: = 6 mason JARS]

FOR A SINGLE DRINK *[handwritten: 100 drinks   (32 ounces per quart)]*

2 ounces vodka *[handwritten ×]*

1 ounce freshly squeezed Meyer lemon juice *[handwritten × 9×]*

1 ounce Honey Syrup (see page 32)

freshly grated zest of 1 Meyer lemon

ice

1 lemon wheel for garnish

Garnish: Lemon wheel

Combine the vodka, lemon juice, Honey Syrup, lemon zest, and ice in a Mason jar and stir until combined.

Garnish with a lemon wheel and serve.

[handwritten: • 200 ounces vodka
100 ounces lemon juice
100 Honey Syrup]

Catch Me *if* You Can

There's an ongoing national shortage of whiskey barrels, and given the increase in bourbon's popularity, you should drink this cocktail before the bourbon runs out.

RECOMMENDED BARWARE

COPPER MUG

¼ cup fresh mint leaves

3 ounces bourbon

¾ to 1 ounce Jalapeño Syrup (see page 34)

Crushed ice

Seltzer water

Garnish: Jalapeño pepper slice and mint leaf

Muddle all but 1 of the mint leaves in a cocktail shaker. Add the bourbon, Jalapeño Syrup, and ice and shake well.

Strain the contents of the shaker into an ice-filled copper mug and top off with the seltzer. Garnish with a jalapeño pepper slice and the remaining mint leaf and serve.

Mama Mia *Punch* SERVES 8

We named this drink after our mamas because we make pitchers of it whenever Mom comes to town. Its vibrant colors make for a beautiful presentation, and its flavors rival any Mimosa or Bloody Mary. As an added bonus, the Mama Mia boasts more nutrients and has fewer calories than the usual brunch favorites.

RECOMMENDED BARWARE

HIGHBALL GLASSES AND A PITCHER

1½ cups freshly squeezed grapefruit juice

1½ cups freshly squeezed orange juice

1 to 1¼ cups vodka

1 cup Honey Syrup (see page 32)

Ice

Seltzer water

Garnish: Lemon, orange, and grapefruit wheels

Combine the grapefruit and orange juices, vodka, and Honey Syrup in a pitcher and stir until well combined.

Pour the contents of the pitcher into 8 ice-filled highball glasses and top off each with the seltzer. Garnish each with lemon, orange, and grapefruit wheels and serve.

FOR A SINGLE DRINK

1½ ounces freshly squeezed grapefruit juice

1½ ounces freshly squeezed orange juice

2 ounces vodka

½ ounce Honey Syrup (see page 32)

Ice

Seltzer water

Garnish: Lemon, orange, and grapefruit wheels

Combine the grapefruit and orange juices, vodka, and Honey Syrup in an ice-filled highball glass and stir until well combined.

Top off with the seltzer. Garnish with lemon, orange, and grapefruit wheels and serve.

The Big Chill SERVES 1

Chili powder is full of vitamin C, which helps boost immunity. Chili powder also has plenty of vitamin A, which helps maintain your collagen levels and the levels of moisture in your hair and skin. Make this cocktail and chill out with college friends you haven't seen in a long time.

RECOMMENDED BARWARE

COUPETTE OR MARTINI GLASS

1 tablespoon chili powder

2 lime wedges

2 ounces silver tequila ✗8 – 16oz

3/4 ounce freshly squeezed ✗8 = 12oz
lime juice

3/4 ounce Ginger Syrup ✗8 = 12oz
(see page 31)

1/4 teaspoon freshly expressed
ginger juice

Ice

Garnish: Lime wedge

Scatter the chili powder on a plate or in a wide, shallow bowl. Rim a coupette or martini glass with 1 of the lime wedges and dip the rim of the glass into the chili powder. Set aside.

Combine the tequila, lime juice, Ginger Syrup, ginger juice, and ice in a cocktail shaker and shake for 10 seconds.

Strain the contents of the shaker into the prepared glass, garnish with the remaining lime wedge, and serve.

4servers ✗ 4 = 16

8 oz. tequila ✗4   32 oz

3 oz. lime juice ✗4   12 oz

3 oz ginger syrup ✗4 = 12 oz

Chapter Six

Fresh *and* Green

Garden *State* SERVES 1

This cocktail is decidedly clean and refreshing. We use cucumbers picked straight from our gardens, and their high water content helps us stay cool during those hot summer months down on the Jersey Shore. Plus, we use the garnish for relief from the sunburns we inevitably get on the beach.

RECOMMENDED BARWARE

ROCKS GLASS

2 fresh mint sprigs

3 tablespoons strained cucumber puree (see page 70)

1½ ounces gin

½ ounce freshly squeezed lime juice

1 tablespoon Honey Syrup (see page 32)

Seltzer water

Ice

Garnish: Cucumber slices, mint leaf, and lime wheel

Muddle the mint sprigs in a cocktail shaker. Add the cucumber puree, gin, lime juice, Honey Syrup, and ice and shake for 10 seconds.

Strain the contents of the shaker into an ice-filled rocks glass. Top off with the seltzer. Garnish with cucumber slices, mint leaf, and lime wheel and serve.

Bloody SophistiKATEd SERVES 4

We love a well-seasoned Bloody Mary, but not the salt and bloat that comes along with the standard Bloody Mary recipe. Our flavorful and colorful twist on this age-old cocktail is the perfect commodity for Sunday brunch. This fun and fresh spin was inspired by one of our favorite wellness experts, Kate Hudson. The Bloody SophistiKATEd makes us "pretty happy."

RECOMMENDED BARWARE

HIGHBALL GLASSES AND A PITCHER

Sea salt

2 lime wedges

Ice

4 green tomatoes, roughly cut

5 tomatillos, husks removed and washed

1 cup vodka

1 cup fresh tomato puree

½ stalk celery, roughly cut

Small handful fresh cilantro

Freshly squeezed juice of 2 lemons

½ teaspoon salt

¼ teaspoon freshly ground black pepper

Garnish: Whole celery stalks, chopped cilantro, and hot sauce (optional)

Scatter the salt on a plate or in a wide, shallow bowl. Rim 4 highball glasses with the lime wedges and dip the rim of the glasses into the salt. Fill the glasses with ice and set aside.

Combine the tomatoes, tomatillos, vodka, tomato puree, celery, lemon juice, cilantro, salt, and black pepper in a powerful blender and process until smooth.

Pour the contents of the blender into the prepared glasses. Refrigerate before serving to chill the cocktail. Garnish each with whole celery stalks, cilantro, and a few dashes of the hot sauce, if using, and serve.

We Got *the* Beet SERVES 1

This is the drink of rock stars! Beets are high in iron, which combats anemia and boosts your energy so you can "go-go."

2 ounces bourbon

1 ounce freshly expressed beet juice

3/4 ounce freshly squeezed lemon juice

1/2 ounce maple syrup

1/4 ounce Ginger Syrup (see page 31)

Ice

Garnish: Ginger coin and lemon wheel

Combine the bourbon, beet and lemon juices, maple syrup, Ginger Syrup, and ice in a cocktail shaker and shake for 10 seconds.

Strain into a coupette glass, garnish with a ginger coin and lemon wheel, and serve.

The All-Night Bender SERVES 1

Packed with beta carotene and antioxidants, this orange wonder-in-a-glass will reduce inflammation, so you're not pie-eyed the morning after.

RECOMMENDED BARWARE

ROCKS GLASS

5 fresh ginger coins

2 ounces gin

1 ounce carrot juice

1/2 ounce freshly squeezed lime juice

1/4 ounce Honey Syrup (see page 32)

Ice

Garnish: Carrot coin and lime wedge

Muddle the ginger coins in a cocktail shaker. Add the gin, carrot and lime juices, Honey Syrup, and ice and shake for 10 seconds.

Strain the contents of the shaker into an ice-filled rocks glass. Garnish with a carrot coin and lime wedge and serve.

Mercury *in* Retrograde SERVES 1

Cilantro is one of the few herbs that can remove heavy metals, like mercury and aluminum, from the body. And as it is with mercury in retrograde, no one can predict where the evening will take you after one or two of these.

RECOMMENDED BARWARE

ROCKS GLASS

1 celery stalk, chopped

¼ cup chopped fresh cilantro leaves

1 ounce freshly squeezed lime juice

2 ounces vodka

1 ounce Honey Syrup (see page 32)

Ice

Garnish: Whole celery stalk and cilantro leaves

Muddle the chopped celery, most of the cilantro leaves, and the lime juice in a cocktail shaker. Add the vodka, Honey Syrup, and ice and shake for 10 seconds.

Strain the contents of the shaker into an ice-filled rocks glass. Garnish with a whole celery stalk and the remaining cilantro leaves and serve.

Wasabi Mary SERVES 6 TO 8

In this drink, wasabi, which is often thought of as the Japanese version of horseradish, is complemented by the cooling qualities of tomato and the kick of a salty pickle. The Wasabi Mary is the perfect addition to a Sunday brunch.

RECOMMENDED BARWARE

HIGHBALL GLASSES AND A PITCHER

¼ cup plus 2 tablespoons freshly squeezed lemon or lime juice

1 tablespoon Worcestershire sauce

½ tablespoon wasabi paste

4 cups low-sodium tomato juice

1¼ cups vodka or gin

Ice

Garnishes: Carrot coins, celery stalks, olives, and pickle spears

Combine the lemon juice, Worcestershire sauce, and wasabi paste in a pitcher and stir until well combined. Add the tomato juice and vodka and stir until well combined.

Pour the contents of the pitcher into 6 to 8 ice-filled highball glasses. Garnish each with carrot coins, celery stalks, olives, and pickle spears and serve.

The Drunken Gardener SERVES 1

We love this cocktail because it offers the fresh flavors of a homegrown garden; it's chock full of fresh bell peppers, basil, and lemons. The unadulterated fresh flavor of the bell pepper juice and the earthiness of the basil are rounded out by the tart lemon. This cocktail is perfect for brunch or a family fun day in the backyard.

RECOMMENDED BARWARE

ROCKS GLASS

2 ounces freshly expressed bell pepper juice

2 ounces vodka

1 ounce freshly squeezed lemon juice

½ ounce Basil Syrup (see page 27)

Ice

Seltzer water

Garnish: Bell pepper slice

Combine the bell pepper juice, vodka, lemon juice, Basil Syrup, and ice in a cocktail shaker and shake for 10 seconds.

Strain the contents of the shaker into an ice-filled rocks glass. Top off with the seltzer, garnish with a bell pepper slice, and serve.

The Seeing Eye **SERVES 1**

Everyone knows that carrots are loaded with carotenoids like beta carotene, which is crucial for preserving eyesight. But one or two of these should do the trick—any more and you might start to see double!

RECOMMENDED BARWARE

HIGHBALL GLASS

2 fresh ginger coins

2 ounces vodka

2 ounces carrot juice

1 ounce apple juice

Ice

Seltzer water

Garnish: Carrot coin

Muddle the ginger coins in a cocktail shaker until they are bruised and juiced. Add the vodka, carrot and apple juices, and ice and shake for 10 seconds.

Strain the contents of the shaker into an ice-filled highball glass. Top off with the seltzer, garnish with a carrot coin, and serve.

Verde Mary   SERVES 6 TO 8

This decidedly fresh and delightful variation on a classic cocktail includes tomatillos, which contain naturally occurring phytochemicals that fight cancer.

RECOMMENDED BARWARE

HIGHBALL GLASSES AND A PITCHER

1¼ to 1½ cups vodka

1½ medium cucumbers, peeled

4 tomatillos, husks removed

1 jalapeño pepper, seeded

Juice of 2 limes

2 garlic cloves

2 tablespoons fresh cilantro

Pinch of sea salt

Ice

Garnish: Lime wedges

Combine the vodka, cucumbers, tomatillos, jalapeño pepper, garlic, lime, cilantro, and salt in a powerful blender and puree until well blended.

Pour the contents of the blender into 6 to 8 ice-filled highball glasses. Garnish each with lime wedges and serve.

Caprese *Cocktail* SERVES 1

This cocktail is so savory, it will leave you craving some crusty bread and packing your bags for Italia. Arrivederci!

RECOMMENDED BARWARE

COUPETTE OR MARTINI GLASS

1½ cups basil leaves

1 small Roma tomato,
cut into wedges

½ cup fresh watermelon chunks

2 ounces vodka

Freshly squeezed juice of ½ lime

½ ounce Basil Syrup
(see page 27)

Ice

Garnish: Lime wedge

Muddle the basil leaves, tomato wedges, and watermelon chunks in a cocktail shaker, making sure that the tomato and watermelon pieces release all of their juices. Add the vodka, lime juice, Basil Syrup, and ice and shake for 10 seconds.

Strain the contents of the shaker into a coupette or martini glass, garnish with a lime wedge, and serve.

The Brain Booster   SERVES 1

Arugula is known to regulate calcium in the brain, which reverses neural damage and improves overall brain health. This cocktail will make you think clearer, so lettuce drink up!

RECOMMENDED BARWARE

COUPETTE OR MARTINI GLASS

1 cup fresh arugula leaves

1 ounce freshly squeezed lime juice

1 ounce Honey Syrup (see page 32)

2 ounces gin

Ice

Garnish: Arugula leaf

Muddle all but 1 of the arugula leaves, the lime juice, and the Honey Syrup in a cocktail shaker. Add the gin and ice and shake for 10 seconds.

Strain the contents of the shaker into a coupette or martini glass, garnish with the remaining arugula leaf, and serve.

Pepper Power *Cocktail* SERVES 1

The bell pepper is the superhero of vegetables, as it's loaded with vitamin D and antioxidants. This surprisingly tasty cocktail combines grapefruit and bell peppers, which are packed with vitamin C, to power up your immune system.

RECOMMENDED BARWARE

CHILLED MARTINI GLASS

½ bell pepper, seeded and cut into rings (about 5)

1 small bunch fresh mint leaves

2 ounces vodka

2 ounces freshly squeezed grapefruit juice

½ ounce freshly squeezed lemon juice

1 ounce Honey Syrup (see page 32)

Ice

Garnish: Bell pepper ring

Muddle 4 of the bell pepper rings and the mint leaves in a cocktail shaker, making sure to extract all of the juices. Add the vodka, grapefruit and lemon juices, Honey Syrup, and ice and shake for 10 seconds.

Strain the contents of the shaker into a chilled martini glass. Garnish with the remaining bell pepper ring and serve.

Turn *the* Beet Around   SERVES 1

This cocktail is loaded with magnesium, potassium, vitamin B, and folate, which improves nerve function. The increased nitrates provided by the beet juice will give you the stamina to turn it upside down.

RECOMMENDED BARWARE

ROCKS GLASS

Sea salt and freshly ground black pepper

2 lemon wedges

Ice

2 ounces gin or vodka

1 ounce freshly expressed beet juice

½ ounce freshly squeezed lemon juice

Garnish: Lemon wedge

Combine the salt and black pepper on a plate or in a wide, shallow bowl. Rim a rocks glass with 1 of the lemon wedges and dip the rim of the glass into the salt and pepper mixture. Fill the glass with ice and set aside.

Combine the gin, beet and lemon juices, and ice in a cocktail shaker and shake for 10 seconds.

Strain the contents of the shaker into the prepared glass. Garnish with the remaining lemon wedge and serve.

The Sludgehammer   SERVES 1

Don't be fooled by the sexy appearance of this deep-magenta cocktail. The betaine in this drink will protect your liver, gently detoxifying and eliminating sludge from your body. Not every drink can be sexy.

RECOMMENDED BARWARE

MASON JAR

2 ounces gin

2 ounces freshly expressed beet juice

1 ounce freshly squeezed grapefruit juice

1 ounce Rosemary Syrup (see page 36)

Ice

Seltzer water

Garnish: Rosemary sprig

Combine the gin, beet and grapefruit juices, Rosemary Syrup, and ice in a Mason jar and stir until well combined.

Top off with the seltzer, garnish with a rosemary sprig, and serve.

Serenity *Cocktail* SERVES 1

Cucumbers are known to reduce cholesterol and to keep your blood pressure low and steady. This green-juice cocktail, which features kale and cucumbers, is a fantastic source of calcium, copper, and vitamins A and C. This cocktail will help you keep calm and carry on.

RECOMMENDED BARWARE

MASON JAR

2 ounces gin

¾ ounce freshly expressed kale juice

½ ounce freshly squeezed lemon juice

½ ounce freshly expressed cucumber juice

½ ounce Honey Syrup (see page 32)

Ice

Seltzer water

Garnish: Thin cucumber slice

Combine the gin, kale, cucumber and lemon juices, and Honey Syrup in an ice-filled Mason jar and stir until well combined.

Top off with the seltzer, garnish with a cucumber slice, and serve.

El Chapo   SERVES 1

Cucumbers are high in water and prevent dehydration which often leads to headaches. This little cocktail may look sweet and innocent, but watch out . . . it's a sneaky little bugger.

Sea salt

1 to 2 lime wedges

½ medium cucumber, diced

½ jalapeño pepper, seeded and sliced into rounds

2 ounces silver tequila

1 ounce freshly squeezed lime juice

½ ounce Honey Syrup (see page 32)

Ice

Garnish: Lime wedge, cucumber spear, and jalapeño slice (optional)

Scatter the salt on a plate or in a wide, shallow bowl. Rim a rocks glass with 1 of the lime wedges and dip the rim of the glass into the salt. Fill the glass with ice and set aside.

Muddle the cucumber, 2 to 4 of the jalapeño slices, and the tequila in a cocktail shaker, making sure that the cucumber and jalapeño slices release their juices. Add the lime juice, Honey Syrup, and ice and shake for 10 seconds.

Strain the contents of the shaker into the ice-filled glass. Garnish with the remaining lime wedge, jalapeño slice, and the cucumber spear, if using, and serve.

- 200 ounces tequila
  50 ounces honey syrup
  100 ounces lime

Peas *of* Mind SERVES 1

They may be small, but peas are mighty little powerhouses. They're loaded with anti-inflammatory properties that combat everything from signs of aging to the onset of Alzheimer's disease.

RECOMMENDED BARWARE

COUPETTE OR MARTINI GLASS

3 tablespoons fresh peas

1 ounce freshly squeezed lemon juice

½ ounce Honey Syrup (see page 32)

2 ounces vodka or gin

Ice

Garnish: Floating pea

Muddle all but 1 of the peas, the lemon juice, and the Honey Syrup in a cocktail shaker until the peas are completely mashed. Add the vodka and ice and shake for 10 seconds.

Strain the contents of the shaker into a coupette or martini glass, garnish with the remaining pea, and serve.

Chapter Seven

Herbs *and* Teas

Bourbon *with* Maple'd Rosemary

SERVES 1

The perfect combination of the tartness of lemon, the sweetness of maple syrup, and the warmth of bourbon makes this cocktail a favorite during the dark days of winter.

RECOMMENDED BARWARE

COUPETTE OR MARTINI GLASS

2 fresh rosemary sprigs

Freshly squeezed juice of ½ lemon

1½ ounces bourbon

1 tablespoon maple syrup

Ice

Garnish: Rosemary sprig

Roll 1 of the rosemary sprigs between your hands to release its oils. Add it to a cocktail shaker, along with the lemon juice, bourbon, maple syrup, and ice and shake.

Strain the contents of the shaker into a coupette or martini glass. Garnish with the remaining rosemary sprig and serve.

$\mathcal{A}$ Royal Fizz   SERVES 1

Basil is at the very core of this refreshing cocktail, which includes loads of tart lemon juice and is spiked with gin. Don't forget the garnish, as the smell of basil and lemon is a crucial part of the experience.

RECOMMENDED BARWARE

ROCKS GLASS

2 ounces gin

2 ounces freshly squeezed lemon juice

1 ounce Basil Syrup (see page 27)

Ice

Seltzer water

Garnish: Basil leaves and lemon wedge

Combine the gin, lemon juice, Basil Syrup, and ice in a rocks glass and stir.

Top off with the seltzer, garnish with basil leaves and a lemon wedge, and serve.

The Berry Jamtini   SERVES 1

Loaded with antioxidants and refreshing flavors, this drink is quite simply
the jam!

RECOMMENDED BARWARE

CHILLED MARTINI GLASS

5 to 8 fresh mint leaves

½ ounce freshly squeezed
lime juice

2 ounces gin

½ teaspoon organic unsweetened
raspberry jam

Ice

Seltzer water

Garnish: Mint leaf

Muddle all but 1 of the mint leaves and the lime
juice in a cocktail shaker. Add the gin, jam, and
ice and shake for 10 seconds, until the jam is fully
incorporated.

Strain the contents of the shaker into a chilled
martini glass. Top off with seltzer, garnish with the
remaining mint leaf, and serve.

Melonade SERVES 1

This light, refreshing, and not-too-sweet cocktail is perfect for poolside parties and hydrating on those hot summer days.

RECOMMENDED BARWARE

ROCKS GLASS

2 ounces fresh watermelon puree

¾ ounce freshly squeezed lemon juice

¼ small cucumber, sliced

5 sage leaves

2 ounces gin

1 ounce Watermelon Syrup (see page 38)

Ice

Seltzer water

Garnish: Sage-wrapped watermelon cube

Muddle the watermelon puree, lemon juice, cucumber, and 4 of the sage leaves in a cocktail shaker. Add the gin, Watermelon Syrup, and ice and shake for 10 seconds.

Strain the contents of the shaker into an ice-filled rocks glass. Top off with seltzer, garnish with the remaining sage leaf and watermelon cube, and serve.

Out *of the* Loupe   SERVES 1

Who doesn't love cantaloupe? This drink is inspired by my grandmother, who always served us cantaloupe when we came to visit. Once I was grown, I made this cocktail for her on our Sunday-afternoon visits. Cantaloupe provides a natural energy booster, and when you're 95, an increase in energy is always welcome. Grandma Tess (or as we called her, Princess) loved the herbal tones of the basil paired with the light flavor of the melon . . . let's face it: she liked to relax with a cocktail.

RECOMMENDED BARWARE

MARTINI GLASS

5 fresh basil leaves, torn in half

Freshly squeezed juice of ½ lime

1 teaspoon Honey Syrup
(see page 32)

2 to 2½ ounces freshly expressed cantaloupe juice

2 ounces silver tequila

Ice

Garnish: Cantaloupe balls

Muddle most of the basil leaves, lime juice, and Honey Syrup in a cocktail shaker. Add the cantaloupe juice, tequila, and ice and shake for 10 seconds.

Strain the contents of the shaker into a glass. Garnish with cantaloupe balls and serve.

Spring *Awakenings* SERVES 1

Basil is anti-inflammatory and antibacterial, and it contains a unique mix of flavonoids that are amazing for your skin. This cocktail tastes like the first day of spring in all its glory.

RECOMMENDED BARWARE

ROCKS GLASS

1 small bunch fresh basil leaves

3 ounces vodka

½ ounce Basil Syrup
(see page 27)

Freshly grated zest of ½ lemon

Ice

Seltzer water

Garnish: Basil leaves and lemon twist

Muddle most of the basil leaves with the vodka, Basil Syrup, and lemon zest in a cocktail shaker. Add the ice and shake for 10 seconds.

Strain the contents of the shaker into an ice-filled rocks glass and top off with seltzer. Garnish with the remaining basil leaves and a lemon twist and serve.

The Spiced SuBourbon SERVES 1

The taste of fall is the star of this simple cocktail. It's a little spicy, a little sweet, and downright warming. This cocktail reminds us of cool fall days and hanging with good friends.

RECOMMENDED BARWARE

MARTINI GLASS

¼ cup freshly squeezed
clementine juice

1 ounce bourbon

2 to 3 whole cloves

Ice

Garnish: Whole clove and
clementine peel (optional)

Combine the clementine juice, bourbon, and all but 1 of the cloves in a cocktail shaker. Add the ice and shake for 10 seconds.

Strain the contents of the shaker into a martini glass. Garnish with the remaining whole clove and the clementine peel, if using, and serve.

Rosemary Greyhound   SERVES 1

This is a festive and flavorful twist on a traditional greyhound that's loaded with vitamin C! Fun fact: Gargling with rosemary is a holistic remedy for a sore throat.

RECOMMENDED BARWARE

ROCKS GLASS

2 ounces freshly squeezed grapefruit juice

3 fresh rosemary sprigs

2 ounces vodka

Freshly squeezed juice of ½ lemon

½ ounce Rosemary Syrup (see page 36)

Ice

Garnish: Rosemary sprig

Muddle the grapefruit juice and 2 of the rosemary sprigs in a cocktail shaker. Add the vodka, lemon juice, Rosemary Syrup, and ice and shake for 10 seconds.

Strain the contents of the shaker into an ice-filled rocks glass. Garnish with the remaining rosemary sprig and serve.

Orange We *a* Matcha SERVES 1

Matcha, a green-tea powder, contains more than 70 times the antioxidants of orange juice and more than 9 times the beta carotene of spinach. The combination of fresh orange juice with the matcha creates a flavor that is sweet and slightly tangy. It also makes for a great-looking cocktail.

RECOMMENDED BARWARE

CHILLED MARTINI GLASS

1 teaspoon matcha tea powder

¼ cup plus 2 tablespoons warm filtered water

10 fresh mint leaves

1 tablespoon Orange Matcha Syrup (see page 35)

½ tablespoon freshly squeezed orange juice

½ tablespoon freshly squeezed lemon juice

1½ ounces bourbon

Ice

Garnish: Orange wheel

Combine the matcha tea powder and water in a bowl and make a paste.

Muddle 8 of the mint leaves in a cocktail shaker. Add the matcha paste, Orange Matcha Syrup, and orange and lemon juices and stir until the matcha paste is dissolved. Add the bourbon and ice to the shaker and shake well for 10 seconds.

Strain the contents of the shaker into a chilled martini glass. Garnish with an orange wheel and serve.

Jalapeño Thai *Iced Tea* SERVES 1

This twist on classic Thai iced tea boasts the addition of spicy Jalapeño Syrup.

RECOMMENDED BARWARE

TALL GLASS

1 cup brewed black tea, cold

1 ounce bourbon

1 ounce Jalapeño Syrup
(see page 34)

Ice

1 ounce almond milk (optional)

Garnish: Jalapeño pepper slice

Combine the tea, bourbon, and Jalapeño Syrup in a tall glass and stir gently. Add the ice and the almond milk, if using.

Garnish with a jalapeño slice and serve.

Calm-omile *Cocktail* SERVES 1

Chamomile is widely known for its sedative effect; it's much like a mild tranquilizer, but is more socially acceptable. Plus, it's tea with honey, so this cocktail will cure your sore throat and make for a sweet slumber.

RECOMMENDED BARWARE

CHILLED COUPETTE OR MARTINI GLASS

2 ounces gin

1 ounce brewed chamomile tea, cold

1 ounce Honey Syrup
(see page 32)

Ice

Garnish: Lemon twist

Combine the gin, tea, Honey Syrup, and ice in a cocktail shaker and shake for 10 seconds.

Pour the contents of the shaker into a chilled coupette or martini glass. Garnish with a lemon twist and serve.

FOR A PITCHER (SERVES 6)

1 cup gin

2 cups brewed chamomile tea, cold

3/4 cup Honey Syrup (see page 32)

Ice

Garnish: Lemon twists

Combine the gin, tea, Honey Syrup, and ice in a pitcher and stir until well combined.

Pour the contents of the pitcher into 6 chilled coupette or martini glasses, garnish each with lemon twists, and serve.

Kiwi *Punch* SERVES 6

A kiwi is packed with more vitamin C and has more antioxidants than an orange. Thanks to the kiwi and mint in this drink, sweet and tart components add a punch to the flavor of green tea.

RECOMMENDED BARWARE

HIGHBALL GLASSES AND A PITCHER

2 medium cucumbers, peeled and quartered

1½ cups fresh mint leaves

6 cups brewed unsweetened green tea, cold

2 kiwis, peeled and sliced

1 cup silver tequila or gin

¾ cup freshly squeezed lemon juice

¼ cup Ginger Syrup (see page 31)

¼ cup Honey Syrup (see page 32)

Pinch of salt

Ice

Garnish: Mint leaves and additional kiwi or cucumber slices

Combine the cucumbers and all but 6 of the mint leaves in a powerful blender and process until smooth. Add the tea, kiwis, tequila, lemon juice, Ginger and Honey Syrups, and salt and process until smooth.

Pour the contents of the blender into 6 ice-filled highball glasses. Garnish each with the remaining mint leaves and additional kiwi or cucumber slices and serve.

> You may want to strain the contents of your blender when pouring into your glasses if you prefer your drink without pulp. We personally enjoy the extra fiber that slows down the absorption of any natural sugars in the drink. To each his own!

Enlighten-Mint Kombucha *Cocktail*

SERVES 1

Kombucha, a fermented drink typically made from either black or green tea, contains enzymes and probiotics that promote gut health. In this drink, we add a little mint for flavor and also as an additional digestive aid.

RECOMMENDED BARWARE

HIGHBALL GLASS

1 small bunch fresh mint leaves

¼ cup fresh raspberries

2 ounces vodka

Ice

½ to ¾ cup cold kombucha tea for topping

Seltzer water

3 dashes Citrus Bitters (see page 43) for topping

Garnish: Mint leaves and raspberries

Muddle most of the mint leaves and all but a few of the raspberries in a cocktail shaker. Add the vodka and ice and shake for 10 seconds.

Strain the contents of the shaker into an ice-filled highball glass and top off with the kombucha tea, seltzer, and Citrus Bitters.

Stir gently. Garnish with the remaining mint leaves and raspberries and serve.

Scoby *Mule* SERVES 1

Kombucha is a fermented beverage produced by a symbiotic colony of bacteria and yeast—otherwise known as a Scoby. Scoby is great for digestive health and far better for you than ginger beer, which is loaded with refined sugars.

RECOMMENDED BARWARE

CHILLED COPPER MUG

2 fresh ginger coins

2 ounces vodka

½ ounce freshly squeezed lemon juice

½ ounce freshly squeezed lime juice

5 dashes Citrus Bitters (see page 43)

Ice

3 ounces cold kombucha tea

Seltzer water

Garnish: Lemon twist

Muddle the ginger coins in a cocktail shaker. Add the vodka, lemon and lime juices, Citrus Bitters, and ice and shake for 10 seconds. Add the kombucha tea and stir for 5 seconds.

Strain the contents of the shaker into a chilled copper mug. Top off with seltzer, garnish with a lemon twist, and serve.

Blooming Jasmine SERVES 6

Jasmine tea, like many of the other teas used in this book, is known for calming moods and lowering heart rates.

RECOMMENDED BARWARE

ROCKS GLASSES AND A PITCHER

8 fresh ginger coins

⅓ cup Ginger Syrup
(see page 31)

1 cup brewed jasmine tea, cold

⅔ cup vodka

1½ ounces freshly squeezed
lemon juice

Ice

Seltzer water

Garnish: Freshly grated ginger

Muddle the ginger coins and Ginger Syrup in a pitcher. Add the tea, vodka, lemon juice, and ice and stir until well combined.

Strain the contents of the pitcher into 6 ice-filled rocks glasses. Top off each with seltzer, garnish with grated ginger, and serve.

FOR A SINGLE DRINK

2 fresh ginger coins

½ ounce Ginger Syrup
(see page 31)

3 ounces brewed jasmine tea, cold

2 ounces vodka

½ ounce freshly squeezed
lemon juice

Ice

Seltzer water

Garnish: Freshly grated ginger

Muddle the ginger coins and Ginger Syrup in a cocktail shaker. Add the tea, vodka, lemon juice, and ice and shake for 10 seconds.

Strain the contents of the shaker into an ice-filled rocks glass. Top off with seltzer, garnish with grated ginger, and serve.

Steep *Thoughts* SERVES 6

Oolong tea is known for boosting mental alertness, due in large part to its caffeine content. Add this drink to your routine for a natural caffeine boost in the early afternoon or in lieu of your morning coffee—just leave out the vodka!

RECOMMENDED BARWARE

MASON JARS AND A PITCHER

2¼ cups brewed oolong tea, cold

1½ cups vodka

2/3 cup Cinnamon Girl Syrup (see page 28)

2/3 cup almond milk (optional)

Ice

Garnish: Cinnamon sticks

Combine the tea, vodka, Cinnamon Girl Syrup, and almond milk, if using, in a pitcher and stir until well combined.

Pour the contents of the pitcher into 6 ice-filled Mason jars, garnish each with a cinnamon stick, and serve.

FOR A SINGLE DRINK

3 ounces brewed oolong tea, cold

2 ounces vodka

1 ounce Cinnamon Girl Syrup (see page 28)

1 ounce almond milk (optional)

Ice

Garnish: Cinnamon stick

Combine the tea, vodka, Cinnamon Girl Syrup, and almond milk, if using, in an ice-filled Mason jar and stir until well combined.

Garnish with a cinnamon stick and serve.

Chapter Eight

Mocktails

You may wonder why we included a chapter on mocktails and booze-free elixirs in a cocktail book. While you're probably reading this book to get healthier recipes for cocktails, you may also find yourself entertaining someone who doesn't drink alcohol at all or is abstaining for a time (perhaps he or she overindulged the night before?). Teetotaling guests need not be relegated to seltzer or soda water—you should be able to offer a special drink to any guest.

If you happen to find yourself with a hangover (it happens to the best of us!), you'll want to check out the elixirs at the end of this chapter. Hangovers can be caused by the use of low-quality alcohol or cheap commercial mixers loaded with refined sugar and additives in your cocktails. But let's be honest—even clean cocktails can give you a headache if you drink too many of them. Only time will completely rid you of the headaches and nausea that are characteristic of hangovers, but we can help speed up the process.

One of the primary causes of the dreaded hangover is dehydration. When you're consuming alcohol, you need to replenish the fluids in your body with lots of water—or, better yet, fresh fruit and vegetable juices loaded with the vitamins your body needs to repair itself. On the following pages, you'll find a few of our favorite remedies for sipping the morning after an overindulgent night out.

Baby-on-Board *Mocktail* SERVES 1

At some point in your life, you'll likely find yourself hosting a pregnant mama. She deserves a special drink, so why not offer her something that's good for her and her bundle of joy? The spinach in this Baby-on-Board Mocktail is loaded with folate, which is critical to the health of any unborn babe, and the pineapple and mint add sweetness. This is a drink she'll feel great about!

RECOMMENDED BARWARE

HIGHBALL GLASS

1 large cucumber, sliced

2 cups diced fresh pineapple

2 cups fresh spinach

1½ cups diced broccoli florets

½ cup fresh mint leaves

½ cup ice

2 ounces freshly squeezed lemon juice

Combine all of the ingredients in a powerful blender and process until smooth.

Pour the contents of the blender into a highball glass and serve.

Designated Diva *Mocktail* SERVES 1

This drink is perfect for your designated-driver friends who are watching their waistlines. The Designated Diva Mocktail is a low-calorie drink reminiscent of the Master Cleanse. The maple syrup in it provides vitamins and minerals, while the cayenne pepper speeds up your metabolism and detoxifies your system.

RECOMMENDED BARWARE

ROCKS GLASS

2 ounces freshly expressed ginger juice

2 ounces freshly squeezed lemon juice

2 ounces cold filtered water

Splash of maple syrup

Pinch of cayenne pepper

Ice

Garnish: Ginger coin

Combine the ginger and lemon juices, filtered water, maple syrup, cayenne pepper, and ice in a rocks glass, stirring gently.

Garnish with a ginger coin and serve.

Clean and Serene *Mocktail* SERVES 6

This drink is the right thing to offer a friend who's on a cleanse or in desperate need of a detox. The active charcoal in the Clean and Serene Mocktail gently removes toxins from your system.

RECOMMENDED BARWARE

HIGHBALL GLASSES AND A PITCHER

½ cup hot filtered water

2 ounces maple syrup

3½ cups very cold filtered water

½ to ¾ cup freshly squeezed lemon juice

½ teaspoon or 1 to 2 open capsules activated charcoal

Pinch of Himalayan salt

Stir together the hot water and maple syrup in a bowl until the syrup is dissolved.

Combine the hot water–maple syrup mixture, very cold water, lemon juice, activated charcoal, and salt in a pitcher and stir until well combined. (This will keep fresh stored in the refrigerator for 3 to 5 days.)

Pour the contents of the pitcher into 6 highball glasses and drink on an empty stomach.

Straight-Edge Punch *Mocktail* SERVES 3

Offer this mocktail to guests who are feeling a little hormonal, manic, or off balance. The turmeric in this cocktail stabilizes your mood, which may be necessary if you're the only sober person at a party.

RECOMMENDED BARWARE

MASON JARS

2 cups brewed green tea, cold

¼ cup raw honey plus more as needed

1 ounce freshly squeezed lime juice

1 ounce freshly squeezed lemon juice

½ ounce freshly expressed ginger juice

2 teaspoons turmeric powder

Pinch of salt

Garnish: Lime wedges

Combine the tea and honey in a pitcher and stir until well combined. Add the lime, lemon, and ginger juices, turmeric, and salt and stir until well combined. Taste for sweetness and add more honey, if desired.

Pour the contents of the pitcher into 3 ice-filled Mason jars. Garnish each with lime wedges and serve.

"Just Say No" Mocktail

SERVES 3

If you've have had too many late nights out, you may have to "just say no." Offer up this minty elixir to guests who just say no, and they won't feel bad about abstaining.

RECOMMENDED BARWARE

HIGHBALL GLASS OR MASON JAR

10 fresh mint leaves

3 fresh sage leaves

8 ounces carrot juice

1/2 ounce freshly squeezed lemon juice

1 teaspoon ground turmeric

Ice

Garnish: Mint and sage leaves

Muddle all but 3 each of the mint and sage leaves in a cocktail shaker. Add the carrot and lemon juices, turmeric, and ice and shake for 10 seconds.

Strain the contents of the shaker into 3 ice-filled highball glasses or Mason jars, garnish each with any remaining mint and sage leaves, and serve.

Oh! Cherry *Mocktail* SERVES 6

This is a great drink to offer sleep-deprived friends who are in desperate need of rest. Tell them to skip the Ambien and instead have a glass of Oh! Cherry. Cherry juice is loaded with melatonin and tryptophan, which helps ensure a sweet night's sleep.

RECOMMENDED BARWARE

HIGHBALL GLASSES OR MASON JARS

3 cups unsweetened cherry juice

6 ounces freshly expressed turmeric root juice

6 ounces Honey Syrup (see page 32)

Ice

Garnish: Cherries

Combine cherry and turmeric juices, Honey Syrup, and ice in a pitcher and stir gently.

Pour the contents of the pitcher into ice-filled Mason jars. Garnish each with a cherry and serve.

The Sun Also Rises
(aka Morning-After) Elixir **SERVES 4 TO 6**

This is the perfect brunch drink for guests who got a bit rowdy the night before. Help them ease the discomfort of their hangovers with this drink, which will restore lost vitamins and fluids.

RECOMMENDED BARWARE

MUG

5 cups filtered water

¼ cup fresh ginger coins

1 cup strong brewed mint tea (using 2 tea bags), cold

Freshly squeezed juice of 1 lemon

1 tablespoon raw honey

½ teaspoon freshly grated turmeric

¼ teaspoon sea salt

Garnish: Lemon wedges

Place the water in a saucepan over medium-high heat and bring to a boil. Reduce the heat to medium-low, add the ginger coins, and simmer for 20 minutes. Remove from the heat.

Add the tea, lemon juice, ginger coins, honey, turmeric, and salt to the saucepan, stir, and set aside to steep for 5 to 7 minutes.

Strain the contents of the saucepan into 4 to 6 mugs, garnish each with lemon wedges, and serve. Drink throughout the day, and make a second batch if needed.

> Why turmeric and ginger? Turmeric is an ancient Indian spice known for its anti-inflammatory properties and positive effects on the liver, the organ responsible for detoxifying the body. Ginger is widely known to be one of the most effective natural remedies for stomach upset. Together, these two are a force to be reckoned with.

If You Like Clean Colada *Elixir*

SERVES 4 TO 6

Escape with our cleaned-up version of a piña colada.

RECOMMENDED BARWARE

HIGHBALL GLASS

2 bananas, peeled

2 cups fresh pineapple chunks

1 cup pineapple juice

1 cup coconut water

1 cup ice

Freshly squeezed juice of 1 lemon

Garnish: Pineapple wedges

Combine all of the ingredients in a powerful blender and process until smooth.

Pour the contents of the blender into glasses, garnish each with a pineapple wedge, and serve.

> Why bananas? One downside of a boozy evening: the many trips you'll take to the bathroom, where you'll not only lose fluids but also potassium. A medium banana is chock full of potassium (approximately 422 mg), which will alleviate the headaches that come with dehydration.

Morning Regrets *Elixir* SERVES 4 TO 6

Occasionally, we are over-served. This feel-good elixir will help you recover and put those morning regrets into perspective.

RECOMMENDED BARWARE

HIGHBALL GLASS

2 fresh limes, cut into wedges

8 fresh mint sprigs

4 cups coconut water

4 cups seltzer water

1 cup ice

Garnish: Mint sprigs

Muddle the lime wedges and most of the mint sprigs in a pitcher. Add the coconut water, seltzer, and ice to the pitcher and stir gently.

Strain the contents of the pitcher into 4 to 6 highball glasses. Garnish each with the remaining mint sprigs and serve.

> Why coconut water? A night out of drinking causes you to lose sodium and electrolytes. Think of coconut water as Gatorade, only healthier and without the artificial flavors and colors. Coconut water delivers a huge dose of electrolytes, which are essential to rehydrate your body.

INDEX

Italicized pages refer to photos.

ABOUT THE AUTHORS

Beth Ritter Nydick

Beth Ritter Nydick's wellness-through-nutrition adventure has led her to be a featured expert on *The Dr. Oz Show*, *The Chew*, and the New Jersey-focused website OMJ.com.

As the founder of Blue Barn Kitchen, a health-focused lifestyle brand designed with a 360-degree approach to health and wellness, Beth helps her clients and readers live life to its healthiest and fullest potential through her creative recipes, simple meal plans, and total lifestyle programs. She is a holistic nutrition and whole-living expert who serves as a supportive voice of reason in a world flooded with fads, tonics, quick-fixes, and diet dilemmas. Beth's healthy recipes and straightforward advice help put healthy living within reach for even the busiest people. She also sells her insanely delicious whole-food bars on her website and in specialty stores in and around New Jersey.

Beth is very active on her own social-media forums and has also appeared as a guest blogger on the website of *The Dr. Oz Show*, the online magazine *Nylon*, and the websites Twiniversity, Skinny Mom, and Womenista.

The former TV producer and Diet Coke addict now lives a healthy, clean lifestyle in New Jersey with her husband; her two teenage boys, Jack and Maxwell; and her adopted pit bull, Spike. She is a holistic health coach certified by the Institute for Integrative Nutrition.

Tara Roscioli

In her work as an attorney, Tara Roscioli learned firsthand how stress can wreak havoc on health and wellness. After living for years on cigarettes, cheap wine, caffeine, and vending-machine food, she decided to defect from the practice of law and see where her gypsy soul landed.

She chose to pursue her passion for healthy living (ironic, given her former diet of Swedish fish and candy corn) and graduated as a certified holistic health coach from the Institute for Integrative Nutrition. For years, she has counseled clients on how clean eating can lead to weight loss, energy gains, and hormone balancing. There's nothing you can say that will shock her!

As the owner of the health-and-wellness practice Highway 2 Well (a name beloved by AC/DC fans everywhere), Tara counsels her clients on how to live a balanced life. She is also the co-owner of the Align Wellness Studio, a Millburn, New Jersey-based Pilates and fitness studio that opened its doors in November 2013.

One of Tara's greatest passions is her plant-based organic meal delivery service, Meals 2 GLO. Tara and her team personally prepare their healthy meals and snacks and deliver them to clients throughout New Jersey, Manhattan, and Brooklyn. Meals 2 GLO continues to grow in recognition and was recently named by Instyle.com as one of its top three favorite meal delivery services.

It's a 24/7 job, but a true labor of love, for Tara and her team!

Tara's health-and-wellness services have been featured in *The Wall Street Journal* and on the web at InStyle.com and PureWow. She has contributed expert advice to multiple articles on Brides.com, *Family Circle*, and *Pilates Style* and has appeared on Fox News. She has also contributed health-and-wellness articles to the enormously popular websites MindBodyGreen and Gaiam.

Tara's other passions include her husband, Jerry; her little boy, Ben; her menagerie of disabled pets, including Lulu, the French bulldog in diapers that zooms about in a wheelchair; all things Tracy Anderson Method; and, of course, a very clean craft cocktail!